Publishing Director
JORDI VIGUÉ

Editor
NORBERTO CALABRÓ

Text
HUGH ALDERSEY-WILLIAMS

First published in Great Britain in 1994 by
Lund Humphries Publishers
Park House, 1 Russell Gardens
London NW11 9NN

**British Library Cataloguing in Publication
Data**
A catalogue record for this book is available
from the British Library

ISBN 0 85331 652 X

Designed by Ricard Badia
Typesetting by TECFA, Spain
Printed and bound in Spain by Gráficas Estella

CORPORATE IDENTITY

BY HUGH ALDERSEY-WILLIAMS

LUND HUMPHRIES
LONDON

CONTENTS

INTRODUCTION

Change. Change affects all of us. In commerce and administration, change affects business at all levels, from giant multinational corporations to public service providers, from small manufacturers to government agencies. All of these organisations must, to a greater or lesser degree, react to change.

A corporate identity is an expression—visual, but also attitudinal—of a company's character. In an unchanging world, a corporate identity would be a constant thing, passed on from year to year down the generations without modification or renewal. But in the rapidly changing world of business, a corporate identity, although a symbol of constancy and reassurance, must also change from time to time.

The case studies that follow are not studies of corporate identities *per se*. They are case studies of changes in corporate identities. In each case, an organisation felt a need to change, often in subtle and deep ways, and also felt a need to express that change with a change of corporate identity.

The range of case studies attempts to cover many manners of commercial activity. From their breadth and diversity, it is hoped that a picture emerges of the changing nature of corporate identity at large. The broadest reach of all is from the commercial concern which has long used corporate identity as a weapon in the battle to gain competitive advantage to the public service provider, which was not until quite recently seen as a user of corporate identity at all.

IDEOLOGIES OLD AND NEW

The line between the public service ethos and the traditional arrogance of the private corporation has become blurred. It will become still more blurred in the future. This is one of the most significant changes now sweeping through large organisations. In the former case, new political ideology drives the change, transforming public service providers into privatised quasi-corporations. In the latter, the change is partly political too as governments have legislated to deregulate formerly restricted markets in the private sector and moved to make private industry more accountable to its customers. But perhaps the more powerful force for change affecting private companies in this respect is the action of the market force wielded by increasingly aware consumers. The combined action of governments and consumers is slowly driving corporations to pursue a more ethical course, not only with regard to the products they make and the way they make them, but also to their staff and the way they are treated. They must examine these practices in order to guard their corporate reputation in a commercial environment where customers are freer than ever to judge one company or product against its competitors on price and performance as always, but also now on political ethics, industrial relations, environmental policy, and other factors.

PRACTICE AND APPEARANCE

It is into this context that a new corporate identity must place itself. The relation between a corporation's practice and its appearance—and particularly between good practice and attractive appearance—is often misunderstood, however.

It is misunderstood by the public, who often distrust the spending of what seems like large sums of money on "cosmetic" changes. It is misunderstood by company staff, who can too easily take a similar position but add a layer of bitterness because they think they know where the money would have been better spent (if not on their salaries).

It is misunderstood most seriously by company managers, who still too often see the adoption of a new corporate identity as a substitute for real change in the behaviour of the company and its staff.

Some of this confusion stems from uncertainty as to what corporate identity really is. The first distinction to be made is between corporate identity—the visual expression of an entire company—and brand identity, which is the expression of a company's trading division or particular product and one of several such identities. In a few instances, the two types of identity are virtually equivalent. In what is effectively seen as a one-product company such as Coca-Cola, the corporate identity is quite deliberately closely related to the identity of its principal brand. This distinction made clear, there are nevertheless different methods of using a corporate identity. Corporations vary in the way they express their identities for good reasons related to the type and range of products that they make. Some manufacturers, such as IBM or Apple Computer, use their corporate identity uniformly on all their products as well as on their literature and company buildings. Others use a corporate identity in conjunction with a range of brand identities. It can suit some to use brand identities in isolation, without support from the corporate identity. This is the case, for example, where a brand is very well known by consumers but the company owning the brand is almost unknown or irrelevant to the consumer (although it will be relevant to a different group, perhaps supplier companies, where the corporate identity will be important).

Corporate identity is important in all these cases. But it is still a poorly defined term. In the narrow sense in which the phrase is routinely used by the design profession, corporate identity is one expression of a company's personality. Other expressions of personality come from the pleasantness or otherwise of staff, the speed and efficiency of action, the company's office or shop environments, the quality of its product design or any of a host of other factors.

The right personality is something that all companies like to have, but frequently their personality is not what they wish for themselves. This is when change becomes necessary. Since a corporate identity is the designed expression of a company's personality, it follows that a real change of personality should be followed by considering a change of corporate identity. It does not follow that a new corporate identity will produce the desired change of personality without other changes also being made.

In most organisations, the corporate identity must address two principal groups: the customers and the staff. (In some cases, it will also be important to influence other groups such as potential advertisers, investors, or

trading partners.) For customers, a successful corporate identity provides a sense of identification. It allows customers to locate that company's shop on a street, or its product on a shelf. It reinforces a feeling already created through customer experience with the product that the customer is willing to seek out that corporate identity in order to purchase that product again. There is growing recognition today that a successful corporate identity can also perform a much needed internal role by giving company staff a sense of identification with the company they work for.

Both customers and staff will know (or find out) when a company's expression of personality—its corporate identity—does not correspond to its actual personality. No corporate identity should seek to disguise a company's real identity. So, if its purpose is not to disguise the truth, as too many executives persist in thinking, what is the purpose of a corporate identity?

PROBLEMS AND PURPOSE

There are a number of problems intrinsic to the design and establishment of a new corporate identity for a company. It must first be established what purpose the new identity is to serve. Given that the corporate identity is an expression of company personality, this means therefore that all parties must be agreed on what the corporate personality was and is to become.

There are a number of entirely conventional reasons for a new expression: the launch of a new company; a merger or acquisition of one company by another; a pronounced change of direction by a company, for example into a new product area or market; diversification; the availability of new markets not anticipated when the previous corporate identity was produced and for which that identity is perhaps inappropriate, for example an opportunity to compete abroad following deregulation. There are many other factors.

The transition of an organisation from the public to the private sector is a special and extreme case. No change could be more complete or abrupt. The wish at the top level to signal that change could hardly be stronger. And yet, in this special case, the introduction of a new corporate identity is especially problematic. The utility undergoing privatisation is often very large, perhaps highly visible throughout the nation. The money spent is seen as being public money. Political expedience often dictates that the change be made very fast—perhaps faster than any equivalent private company would attempt.

In all corporate identity, timing is crucial. It has been stated that a corporate identity is an expression of a company's personality and thus that a new corporate identity should express a change in personality. The true picture is not so simple. In some cases, it is advantageous to introduce the new identity ahead of the more substantial changes that will modify the corporate personality. In others, it would be foolish to make the visible change before the underlying changes had been made and recognised in their own right. A new identity signifies partly a change that has been made, partly further change to come. If no real change has been made or is intended to be made, then a new identity will not disguise the fact for long. If, on the other hand, the changes that have been made by the time a new corporate identity is introduced are the sum of the changes intended to be made, then the company may well squander the catalytic effect which the arrival of its new identity can have in its market.

PUBLIC AND PRIVATE

Turning now to the case studies themselves, these are divided equally between the public (or formerly public) and private sectors. The acute changes—and equally acute difficulties—faced by the public service providers are addressed in studies of the British Broadcasting Corporation and London Underground. The publicly funded BBC faced the need to appear less institutional following changes among commercial broadcasters in Britain. In the long term, it faces the uncertainty of not knowing where its funds, presently obtained by a government levy on the public, are to come from. The London Underground rail network remains publicly owned and comparatively poorly funded. It maintains an environment where design provides not only a competitive advantage but also makes a very real contribution to the provision of a safe and efficient service. It too faces the distant prospect of privatisation.

Studies of BT, formerly the national telephone service British Telecom, and the PTT, the equivalent organisation in Holland, provide strongly contrasting examples of the introduction of new corporate identities following privatisation. BT wished to distance itself from its past, and show a dramatically new personality for an ambitious company intent on breaking into the lucrative international telecoms market. The Dutch PTT, on the other hand, wished to signal a degree of continuity with its past, not least with a reputation for artistic patronage. The results are two identities which can fairly be described as marketing-led in the former case and design-led in the latter.

The final public sector case study reveals the extent to which the essentially commercial practice of corporate design has penetrated into the highly institutional world of government administration. The Délégation Générale de l'Armement of the French Ministry of Defence is a little known organisation that, perhaps surprisingly given its purpose, wants to become better known. Its new corporate identity makes visible a commitment to public service that one way or another is the *raison d'être* of all government offices.

The five private companies featured show on the whole a more subtle approach to corporate identity. This is not surprising, for while public sector organisations are new to the subject, the commercial sector has long understood and made good use of corporate identity. Here, therefore, the requirement is for greater subtlety in the deployment of a visual language that will help each company achieve its aims.

These companies range from the very large to the quite small and from the highly diversified to the very focused. All, however, find themselves in a competitive environment where they need a sophisticated corporate identity—one that will distinguish them from their competition, but not so much that it looks as if they belong in a completely different market.

The case of Bowater, a major print and paper conglomerate, presents the classic corporate identity consultant's problem. Bowater has its fingers in many pies, most of them next to impossible to visualise. Although its public profile is low, it is a very large international organisation for which a powerful corporate identity is important in building a sense of identity among member companies and ensuring recognition from industrial suppliers and customers.

A new puzzle is posed by the rapidly growing and diversi-

olivetti

ptt

fying financial services industry. These companies deal in the most abstract of commodities—paper money in the form of pensions, insurance policies and investment programmes. There is no product that these companies make, so their only visible expression becomes their corporate identity. Alongside other aspects such as the manner of the staff who serve the public, this is one aspect of a corporate personality that is the principal competitive weapon of these companies. The subject of the case study, Nippon Life Insurance Company or Nissay, is one of the very largest such companies practising and competing in this highly abstract field.

Two very different small companies illustrate the fact that corporate identity is no longer only for the largest corporations. At this level, where research is often informal at best and where consultancy budgets are necessarily limited, there is a widespread feeling that a new corporate identity is nothing more than a new symbol or logotype. Unfortunately, some design consultancies perpetuate this misunderstanding by providing such symbols and logotypes and calling them corporate identities. The examples of the British publisher Faber and Faber, and the German type foundry Berthold, show how a more mature understanding of what corporate identity can do has benefited both companies. In the case of Faber, the corporate identity includes a symbol and logotype but also a flexible creative policy regarding the design of its books for the public. Berthold, on the other hand, uses an elegant and understated design vocabulary to address a knowledgeable specialist market.

The Italian computer manufacturer, Olivetti provides a further example of the mature treatment of corporate identity thoroughly integrated with other aspects of corporate expression from cultural events sponsorship to excellently designed products.

CONTENT AND STYLE

Different companies adopt different strategies for their styles of visual expression. BT and Nissay have strong symbols and logotypes that are applied relentlessly to build awareness of the company among the public.

Increasingly, however, corporations are pursuing a more fragmented style in which the corporate identity is composed of a variety of design elements—typefaces, styles of design and illustration, as well as simple, unchanging marks. The visual devices employed by Bowater work, for very good reason, with the Bowater name but also with other names. They have the potential to be used in a variety of inventive ways.

Faber's corporate identity is one of those that is confused with brand identity. The appearance of its books, which includes the Faber symbol, a standard typographic cover treatment, and a certain approach to illustrative artwork, comprises a flexible framework within which designs can be created that are individual and yet expressive of the same corporate identity.

The corporate identity of the Dutch company PTT is a sophisticated kit of parts. The BBC2 identity is made up of a family of symbols with shared characteristics. All these corporate identity systems make provision for subsequent design consultants to create designs for specific projects within the identity guidelines. This approach is indicative of corporations' increasing understanding of and confidence in the design professions. The case studies provide evidence that these companies intend to continue to make use of the best available design as an ingredient for their commercial success.

BBC: PUBLICLY FUNDED NATIONAL TELEVISION BROADCASTER

Client:
British Broadcasting Corporation, London, Great Britain

Corporate identity and design:
Lambie-Nairn and Company, London, Great Britain

Year:
1990

to make the BBC's two television channels appear fresher and less institutional following changes among commercial stations; to safeguard the perception of the BBC as the provider of quality television in Britain

The **BBC1** and **BBC2** symbols identify "brands" under the **BBC** corporate identity designed by **Michael Peters**

The old **BBC1** identity created in-house by the **BBC** made more direct use of the globe as a symbol of the **BBC's** world-wide authority

The old **BBC2** identity used the televisual colour clichés of red, green and blue in a weak white-on-white design

The British refer colloquially to their national broadcasting organisation, the BBC, as "Auntie". The epithet is a telling one. It reveals a certain fondness, but also more ambivalent feelings. "Auntie" is rather formidable; she knows what's best for her little nieces and nephews, the British people.

There is as a result a justifiable pride in a broadcasting company that has done so much to shape the minds of succeeding generations. But this sometimes spills over into complacency. "British television is the best in the world" is a frequently heard phrase, often made as an assertion of faith as much as a statement of fact. The BBC has immense strengths (measured against almost any broadcasting company, public or private, or indeed against other types of public services), but its strengths are also its weakness. It is seen by some as overstaffed, overweening and overconfident.

In presentation terms, the BBC has in the past made do with its avuncular air of authority. Its principal rival, the independent mainstream broadcast television network ITV, has simply muddled through. Two visual cultures

are now forcing both to change. The first is the recent tide of slick retail design and corporate identity that has struck Britain. The second is the startlingly high standard of direction, production and graphics of some British television advertising. The need to smarten up its on-air appearance comes at a time when the corporation faces increased competition from satellite television and an everpresent threat that its public funding may not be guaranteed in the future.

In response to these developments, the British Broadcasting Corporation had already acquired a new corporate identity from Michael Peters and Partners during the 1980s. A new look at television graphics on the corporation's two national channels, BBC1 and BBC2, was a logical next step.

It fell to Pam Masters, a former BBC employee who returned to the corporation from Channel Four, the second independent channel, to take this step. Both BBC1 and BBC2 had new controllers at this time, respectively Jonathan Powell and Alan Yentob. As the newly appointed Head of Presentation, Masters commissioned research from Lambie-Nairn and

The two colours—indigo for **BBC**1 and viridian for **BBC**2—are chosen partly on technical criteria. They must convert into broadcast signals reliably to be

identical in all screen uses as well as close to printed matter colour reproduction

On the rare occasions that the two brands appear together, they are separated by a vertical rule

Company on how the channels were perceived by the public. BBC2 emerged as "weak" and "negative". BBC1 looked better, but was old-fashioned, "a little 'Days of the Raj'," says Masters.

Neither channel at that time employed the new BBC corporate logotype, which is widely disliked. Personal tastes aside, it was clearly proper that the BBC channel identities—the aspect of the BBC that the public sees most often—should carry the identity of the Corporation as a whole. Integrating the overall corporate identity with channel identities became part of the brief.

TRADITION AND INNOVATION

On the basis of the research, it was decided that BBC1 should build on and bring up to date the good aspects of its channel identity, while BBC2 should wipe the slate clean and create a new image appropriate to the change of direction planned for the channel by Yentob.

For reasons of internal politics and visual excellence, Masters looked at what the BBC's substantial in-house

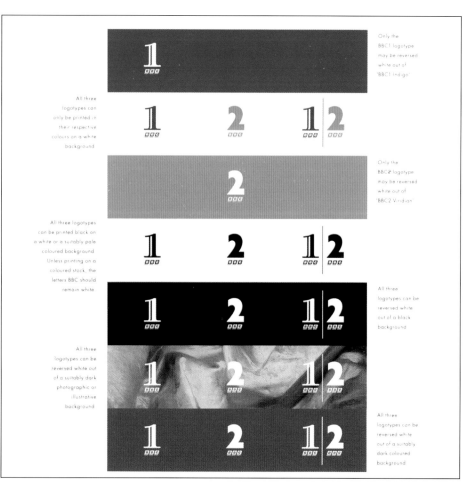

A page from the BBC's "Guidelines for use and reproduction of the **BBC**1 and **BBC**2 channel logotypes" showing the variety of colour usage

Single images trailing individual programmes are also displayed in conjunction with the channel identity stripe

The schedule of forthcoming programmes is displayed in a box with a vertical
bar carrying the appropriate channel
numeral and fragments of the animated
sequence background

TUESDAY

1.00 One O'Clock News
1.30 Neighbours
1.50 Going for Gold
2.15 Outcast of the Islands
3.50 Children's BBC

SPITFIRE!

OLYMPICS 92

Special artwork is created by BBC
designers to advertise some programmes. These too are used in co-ordina-
tion with the channel identity

PORRIDGE

A variety of different still images captu-
red from the channel identity sequence
are used with programme trailer images

graphics staff might be able to produce as well as at external consultants'
work. A handful of firms were invited
to take part in a credentials pitch,
and from these three were selected
to give a creative presentation. The
three were the BBC's in-house graphic design team, led by Brendon Norman-Ross, and consultants Lambie-
Nairn and Company and English,
Markell and Pockett, both of which
have founders who are former BBC
employees.

The television graphic design commu-
nity is a small one. Masters knew
each group well. She had employed
Lambie-Nairn to produce the colourful computer graphics "4" for Channel
Four, an identity still in use ten years
after the channel was launched, a
very long time for a television image.
Once again, Lambie-Nairn got the
job. "It was felt that the work they
produced was visually the most interesting and arresting. We felt they
could cope with the size of this job,"
says Masters.

Lambie-Nairn's proposal centred on
the representation of the channel
numbers in letters: O, N, E and T, W,
O. This created a sense that the two
channels were brother and sister

while still leaving ample opportunity
for variations. For the T, W, O there
was provision for a series of identities using the three letters in different
contexts. Both the letters O were to
contain globes, a revision of old
BBC1 imagery that portrayed a rotating globe, evidence of "Auntie's" rather grandiose world view.

BRANDING VERSUS CORPORATE IDENTITY

At the core of both Masters' and
Lambie-Nairn's thinking lay the perceived need to create brand identities for the two BBC channels under
the umbrella of the Peters corporate
identity. In a press release accompanying the unveiling of the two new
identities in February 1991, Pam Masters explained: "In the more competitive broadcasting landscape of the
1990s, it is essential that BBC Television's 'branding' and corporate identity are strong and present a unified
image."

*But it is hard to draw a meaningful ana-
logy between a manufacturing or trading
company (with a corporate identity and
branded products) and a public broad-*

Both **BBC** channels have a "house" clock, electronically created on screen using elements of the channel identity style

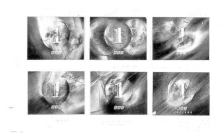

Storyboard sketches prepared by the designers preparatory to constructing the animated sequence

casting service. What is the product? Is it the channels or the programmes? Certainly the programmes and often rival channels are far easier to tell apart than conventional branded consumer products such as soap powder or petrol, so the need for branding is perhaps minimal. Lambie-Nairn's work, therefore, is something of a hybrid.

"We call it a brand identity to mean something wider than a corporate mark," says Lambie-Nairn account director Sarah Davies. "The brand identity usually has to express personality more than a corporate identity."

More important than the legitimacy of the branding argument is that the channel identities should be congruent with what is broadcast on those channels.

"Audiences will understand whether a design is true to a channel," says Brendon Norman-Ross. "Programme content is becoming more graphic and viewers are becoming much more astute in the way they understand the quality of a programme, a script, a piece of design. They will interpret the design."

Ian St John, Managing Director at Lambie-Nairn, feels the branding trend will make British television even more polished than that elsewhere.

"There's no other country that I know of where television is sufficiently developed for what we do to be seen as something that needs to be done."

The final designs produced by Lambie-Nairn are based on greater simplicity for the numerals 1 and 2 rather than the letters O, N, E and T, W, O.

"Complicated designs tend to look dated very quickly," says Martin Lambie-Nairn. "Many years' experience in branding has taught us that starting from a strong and simple mark provides the greatest opportunity for creating lively and exciting on-screen imagery while maintaining the power and integrity of the brand identity."

Martin Lambie-Nairn and Pam Masters worked closely together to ensure that the needs of all interested parties were served. The channel controllers, Powell and Yentob, made regular contributions as the design work progressed. The BBC's director of corporate affairs oversaw compatibility of the broadcast identities with the corporate identity.

"Fibre optics" is an addition to the "2" family designed by the BBC itself although very much in the spirit of the Lambie-Nairn work

"Powder" is another new version of the BBC2 identity created by the BBC's own designers

The notion that the two identities should be seen as brother and sister remains of central importance. Both channels are denoted by single numerals, both centred on screen, both in their own distinctive, unique typeface, and both associated exclusively with their own colour, indigo for BBC1, viridian for BBC2. The two identities have a designed lifetime to the end of the 1990s, but the numerals and their identifying colours may outlive this to be reincarnated as elements in a new live or animated identification sequence.

FAMILY OF LOGOTYPE SEQUENCES

The family nature of the two identities is enhanced by the visual vocabulary used to support them. Both channels have common clock, programme schedule, and special announcement formats. Both use the Futura typeface, because it is easily read on-screen and off and is neither traditional nor modish. The initial thought had been to use a different typeface on each channel. As work progressed however, it was realised that this "branding" would be

too strong. Written messages, such as those advertising an evening's programmes, appear in a very secondary role to the numeral identities themselves. Thus, as Davies explains:

> *"If the message hasn't got over by the time you're reading the type, then you've failed."*

The BBC1 sequence is comparatively safe. It develops the imagery that was present before, retaining the trademark rotating globe. The gradualism signifies that BBC1 will continue to stand for its values. Centred below the number 1 is the identity for the Corporation overall. This identity, the three upper-case italic letters B, B, C in italic boxes with red, green and blue underlining stripes, is an updated version of the Corporation's 1950s lettering. Its dynamic appearance looks right in a mobile context such as on an outside broadcast van, and works adequately in print, but it is positively awkward to deal with on the small rectangle of a television screen. The question was raised of whether to start again from the very top of the organisation and commission a new corporate identity, but this was rejected on grounds of cost

The basic clock design is the same as for **BBC1**, but the colours and lighting echo the **BBC2** identities

Different family members of the **BBC2** identity are used in the vertical channel identification bar

When the occasion merits, the rule of the screen grid can be broken, for example when the programme artwork is of unusual proportions

Stills advertising programmes are accompanied by the 2 numeral on a plain black bar

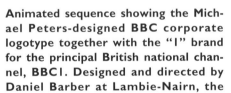

Animated sequence showing the Michael Peters-designed BBC corporate logotype together with the "1" brand for the principal British national channel, BBC1. Designed and directed by Daniel Barber at Lambie-Nairn, the **sequence shows a combination of models and computer animated images of the planet swirling around the numeral in a softened version of the old BBC1 channel identification which showed a rotating globe**

and because the Peters logotype was still very new.

Lambie-Nairn's research had shown people recognised BBC2's reputation for experimentation, high quality, and informative programming, but also that they found it dull, boring and old-fashioned. The designers' final BBC2 identity successfully accentuates the positive qualities and unquestionably eliminates these negatives.

Unlike the BBC1 sequence, this logotype sequence exists in several forms which are in use at the same time. Their names reveal inherent qualities of substance and artistry: "sign", "copper", "water", "silk", "paint", "blade", etc. The sequences are used randomly, although some correlation can be made with various types of programme. Masters explains that, for example, the "water" sequence is playful, while "silk" is more serious. These interpretations are highly subliminal, however, and there are few real rules. It could seem inappropriate, for example, to run the "blade" sequence before a documentary about domestic violence or to use the slightly slapstick "paint" sequence in which paint drops from right to left

Special versions of the **BBC2** identity succeed best where they retain the simplicity and boldness of the original, as with this version for a season of programmes about Japan

onto the 2 (the camera has been turned on its side) before a particularly serious programme.

More sequences will be added gradually while others are dropped, maintaining a constant library of image sequences that bear the family genes—the 2 and the viridian. The first two additions, 18 months after the identity debut, are "fibre optics" and "powder". These are fresh and entertaining, but still clearly within the ground rules established for the sequences. It comes as something of a surprise to learn that they were created not by Lam-bie-Nairn's designers but in-house by the BBC. These rules are vague; there is an emphasis on real materials and live action as opposed to computer graphics (an enduring obsession on American television, but felt by the BBC to be passé). There is no animation, no impression of expensive high-tech tricks. Unusually for new corporate identities, the BBC2 sequences have acquired something of a following.

"They are liked because they are felt to be honest and real," says Davies. "Everyone has a favourite."

For BBC2, a channel characterised by high-quality arts and documentary programmes, Daniel Barber and Martin Lambie-Nairn created a family of identities. The common elements are the bold 2 numeral and the identifying viridian colour. The interpretation uses a variety of tangible materials in a deliberate attempt to escape from clichés of computer graphics:

"Sign" uses flashing neon bulbs in the manner of an illuminated street sign

"Copper" has a corroded antique surface from which sparks fly during the animation

"Water" ripples gently across the screen diagonal, to background music. All sequences have slightly eerie music or sound effects

"Silk" blows in the breeze during this sequence. Textured materials were a key element in the family identity

In "Paint", a splash of viridian drops in surreal fashion from right to left across a block model of the 2 numeral

"Blade" has the 2 numeral cut out of a sheet of steel dropping from out of the screen and coming to rest embedded in the viridian surface

SYNTHESIS

1ambie-Nairn devised separate identities for the two **BBC** channels, related by their use of the appropriate channel numeral. The mainstream **BBC1** combines a "1" with an image of the rotating globe retained from the previous identity to reinforce the **BBC**'s remit to cover world events. **BBC2**, a channel for arts programmes, is more complex, with nine sequences which share the numeral "2" and an aquamarine colour. Through their use of different materials, animation and live action sequences they appear both recognisable and entertainingly varied.

BERTHOLD: DIGITAL PHOTOTYPESETTING

Client:
BERTHOLD, Berlin, Germany

Corporate identity and design:
METADESIGN, Berlin, Germany

Year:
1984–present

brief: To maintain the integrity of the corporate identity while freeing it from an existing rigid format in order to reflect the increasingly eclectic use of typography in design today

Cover for "Die ganze Lösung", a general brochure describing the "all-in-one solution" of Berthold's printing system

Cover for "Berthold zeigt Bild + Farbe". The design plays with process colours, grey shades and image reproduction techniques

BILD

EIGT + *Farbe*

The red box of the Berthold identity has long been the centrepiece of the type foundry's corporate identity

On Berthold literature such as this invitation, the red bar is manipulated to turn covers and run vertically as well as horizontally

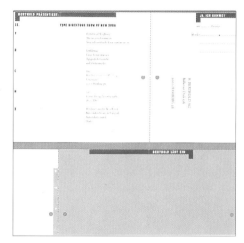

Berthold stationery features the time-honoured red box but also MetaDesign's innovation of the red bar to carry additional information

berthold is and has long been a hallowed name among graphic designers. For more than 130 years this Berlin type foundry has set the standard for typographical excellence which the rest of the world seeks to emulate. Between the two world wars in particular, when it was Europe's largest type foundry, Berthold spearheaded the modern movement in typography.

At the end of 1984, H. Berthold AG asked the typographer and graphic designer Erik Spiekermann of the Berlin consultancy MetaDesign to advise on its presentation in a market that had been revolutionised and expanded greatly by sweeping changes in print and production technologies. The last change of identity had been in the late 1960s, bringing Berthold into the era of photosetting. The requirement now was to signal Berthold's intention to play a leading role in the new revolution of digital typesetting.

There followed a year-long collaboration between MetaDesign and Berthold. The starting point for the work was never a fundamental redesign of Berthold's corporate image, but more a fine-tuned revision of all aspects of the company's visual presentation from the basic tools of its trade to exhibition stands.

Up to now, Berthold had survived without the need for a corporate identity manual or similar book of rules, relying instead on a general understanding that the company's visual image should remain sufficiently open to be able to accommodate developments in design and yet still be unambiguously recognisable. Central to this rather informal credo lay the knowledge that Berthold customers are visually literate people who quickly tire of conventional "corporate design" with all its stifling restrictions.

This feeling that everyone—the client, its customers and its corporate identity design consultant—were on the same side contributed to the smooth running of the project.

"Apart from good designers, good design demands equally good clients. Luckily, this was the case with Berthold," says Spiekermann.

Manfred Pfuhl, then Berthold's director of marketing communication, was both the client and an invaluable discussion partner for all ques-

The inside covers of the 2:1 format "Berthold Programmbibliothek" when seen together reassemble to form the Berthold red box

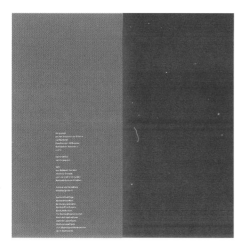

"Die ganze Lösung" inside spread layout. The high technology of modern printing is made accessible through cartoon-like illustrations

tions concerning the Berthold identity. Three MetaDesign staff worked on the Berthold project from the beginning: Hans Werner Holzwarth, Jens Kreitmeyer and Theres Weishappel. Alexander Branczyk and Thomas Nagel continue that work today as MetaDesign creates further items of company literature.

NOSTALGIA FOR THE PRINTER'S CRAFT

Berthold's house colours remain the traditional colours from the history of book-making—the typographer's "colours", black and white (and shades of grey) and touches of red used for ornament or emphasis in the manner of the rubric of illuminated manuscripts from before the invention of the printing press. There is also a more modern allusion to Suprematist art with its abstract compositions in red, black, white and grey.

Berthold's logotype had been a well known red square with the word Berthold reversed out in white. This has been in use for 25 years since the advent of photosetting, first with the

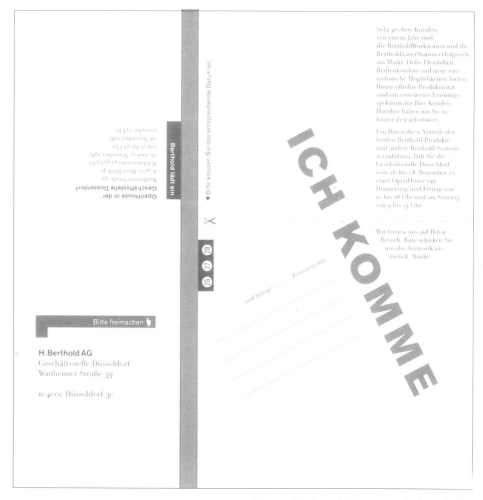

The red is invariable, a reminder of the rubric in illuminated manuscripts. The only other colour is provided by lettering in grey

"Berthold zeigt Bild + Farbe" inside spread layout. The brochure discusses the conversion of images to achieve a variety of desired effects

words "berthold fototype" in the box, then with "berthold", and, finally, from 1988, with "Berthold". Spiekermann says the capital B is a signal that Berthold is "grown up now".

This has been retained by MetaDesign, appearing in most literature exactly 25 mm square, and used as the basis for a system of variations. *The square box itself is never abused, but the same idea is now employed with the use of a red bar on company literature.*

> "The red bars are Berthold-like," says Pfuhl, 'but they are only part of graphic design. There isn't any other registered trademark than the red box."

This bar variously appears with a thickness of one half or one third that of the 25 mm side of the parent Berthold red box. Like the red square this is a sacrosanct mark of recognition, even though it may or may not be used to carry type and is not limited to the horizontal orientation. The bar may drop from the top of a page or run down the side. Like the white Berthold lettering in the red square, the red bar is a carrier of additional proprietary information, for example,

"BertholdPresseinformation" for press releases or "DIE BERTHOLD PROGRAMMBIBLIOTHEK" for a catalogue of typography software.

When it appears without the word Berthold or any other words, the red bar is merely a more subtle indication of Berthold's presence. Sometimes the bar is chopped into short segments that are mini versions of the Berthold red square, providing a further clue as to the identity of the company whose literature it adorns.

More subliminal still is the arrangement of the red bar to describe a halved T. This motif appears frequently both as a decorative and as a linking element. In some orientations, this serves as an arrow to direct attention to particular points in company literature. But oriented so that it appears as the stem and half the crossbar of a capital letter T, it signifies Type and Typography.

For typography is, of course, Berthold's business. It comes as no surprise then to discover that the other principal ingredient of the company's identity in addition to the "rubric" device should be a house typeface. There are nearly 400 typefaces in the Berthold catalogue, ranging from gro-

The "Berthold Type Collection" cover. The book contains more than 200 pages of Berthold typefaces ranging from the modern to the medieval

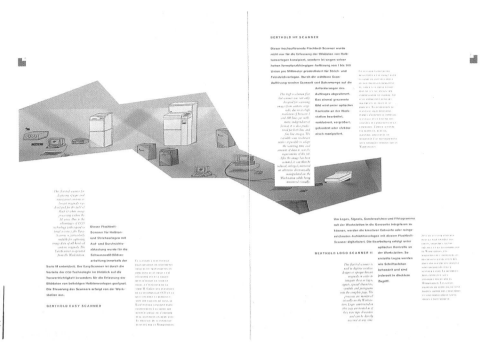

Inside spread layout for "Die ganze Lösung". Three languages are set in different typefaces presenting different grey blocks

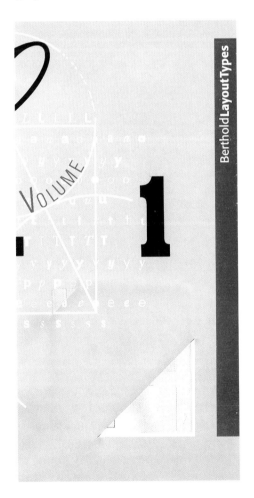

Cover of "Berthold Layout Types", a catalogue supplied with a computer diskette that describes 400 Berthold electronic typefaces

tesk to antiqua (respectively sans serif to serif), from ornate to functional, from the script-like to the constructed, bold and light, expanded and condensed.

A FONT AMONG FONTS

From this dazzling array, MetaDesign and Berthold selected the Akzidenz Grotesk family as the house typeface. The earliest of these fonts dates from the turn of the century and is thus, as Spiekermann puts it, the "mother of Helvetica". Of all the type designs exclusive to Berthold, according to MetaDesign, this family is something of a foundation, suitable for many uses from labelling equipment to proclaiming company names.

Consistency in typography and in other seemingly minor matters is particularly important, says Spiekermann. First impressions are made not from focused attention on a central aspect but from unconcentrated glances, for example, from a fleeting glimpse of some printed matter. A precision approach not only to the elements of typography but also to pictures and to the composi-

tional grids for page layout is as important as the more obvious elements in revealing the company identity. Spiekermann's approach to design and layout is not dogmatic.

Page grids should be interpreted freely, he says, rather than slavishly filled.

The design of Berthold's forms, for example, is based rather romantically on the hot-metal typesetter's tray full of lead type rather than on an entirely abstract grid.

"Isn't a well laid out form one that it is also fun to fill in?" asks Spiekermann. "The comparison with financial bureaucracy should be avoided."

And although Akzidenz Grotesk is the house typeface, other, quite different typefaces, even ornate serif fonts, can play a useful role, while typefaces that have become a cliché in their habitual context have a pleasing freshness in another context. To illustrate the point, Spiekermann permitted himself the designer's conceit of creating quite anomalous numerals for use with the light Akzidenz Grotesk face of company literature. These numerals are non-lining (eg the 6 rises above the line height while

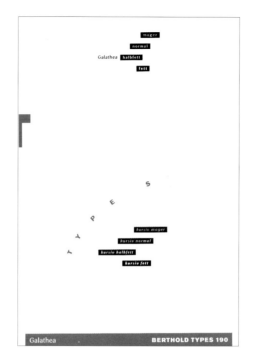

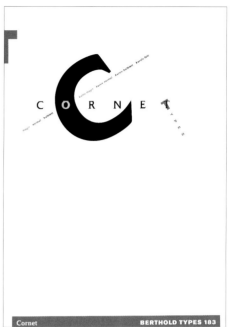

Brochure for the Berthold typeface Galathea. On the spine of each of these brochures is a half T to suggest the word "Type" or "Typography"

Brochure for the Berthold typeface Cornet. The red T makes an additional appearance with the word "Types"

the 7 drops below it) in an "antique" style.

Any of the hundreds of exclusive Berthold fonts may be used in an appropriate context.

"Looser, but still deliberate, insertion of spatial elements such as bars, areas, white space, and the signal and decorative red colour leads to an effect of renewed recognition that avoids the perpetual repetition of the red square on each printed piece" says Spiekermann.

These freedoms are granted most notably for special events such as trade fairs when individual new logotypes may be developed to suit the occasion. Literature produced for a recent Drupa, the printing industry trade fair, for example, took as its subject the liberation of type from the rectangular grid, celebrating the ability of computers to manipulate type in changing sizes, along curves and in three dimensions with a composition of flying type elements.

However, much of MetaDesign's continuing work for Berthold is in the form of the booklets produced to display specimens of each font. More

"Berthold Programmbibliothek" inside spread layout. The brochure describes tools that allow Berthold typefaces to be manipulated and distorted

Inside front cover page introducing Chasseur as a typeface with "beauty and value"

Inside front cover page introducing the Arbiter typeface as "fashionably elegant"

than 50 such brochures have so far been produced.

"Specimen booklets represent a company like Berthold more than anything else, considering that their name is synonymous with the best typefaces available for professional typesetting systems," says Spiekermann.

Each booklet is set entirely in the typeface in question and laid out to show sample blocks of text in this typeface and its italic and bold variants. The covers give slightly greater creative rein. The red bar appears centred at the bottom of the page with white type "BERTHOLD TYPES" and the catalogue number and name of the typeface. On the white ground of the remainder of the cover appear greatly enlarged letterforms together with a list of the weights available in the booklet's typeface. The word "TYPES" appears in red, and at various heights along the bound edge so does the red half–T motif. Like all of Berthold's literature, this work is produced using Berthold's products and equipment. These days this range covers not only type but also graphics and photographs, and colour as well as black and white.

Spread from "The Berthold Type Collection" showing the company's exclusive Akzidenz Grotesk typeface that it uses as its house font

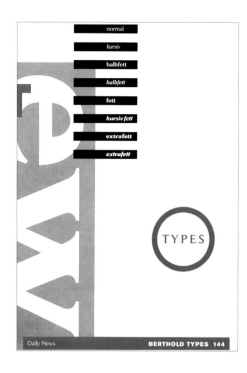

Brochure for the Berthold typeface Daily News

Samples of the Daily News typeface from the brochure

VARIABLE VISUAL ELEMENTS

For external presentation purposes, Berthold places great importance on a style composed of such variable visual elements rather than a free-standing repeated corporate identity. The hard part of this approach is to resist the temptation to increase the number of visual elements beyond that which would look elegant simply in order to ensure that people do recognise the company presence. Spiekermann is adamant, however, that economy in the use of all design elements is a necessity. Generous areas of blank paper—whether white or coloured—are used to bring out the qualities of the type to their fullest.

Berthold's reputation for quality over 130 years has embued its products with an aura of exclusivity even among people who have never worked with Berthold systems. During this time, Europe has witnessed many influential design movements: Constructivism, Neue Sachlichkeit, De Stijl, Dada etc. Berthold occupies an important position in this cultural history. Pfuhl states Berthold's position as being one of "no compromises in typography and graphic design. I think that's the difference between the USA and Germany."

Today, however, the mixing of European typographic cultures made possible by technological advances must find an expression in the corporate image. Spiekermann's strategy makes this change by freeing the Berthold style from mere imitation of well known Bauhaus-style precursors to reflect the eclecticism of a more pluralistic age.

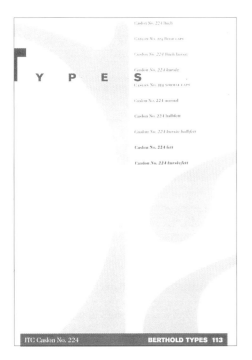

Brochure for the Berthold typeface ITC
Caslon No 224

Brochure for the Berthold typeface
Amalthea

Brochure for the Berthold typeface
Serifa

Brochure for the Berthold typeface
Chasseur

Brochure for the Berthold typeface
Berling

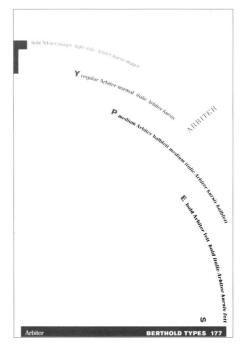

Brochure for the Berthold typeface
Arbiter

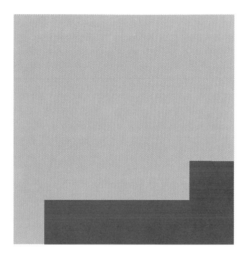

Detail of the front cover of the "Bert-hold Programmbibliothek" showing the half–T motif which serves as an invitation to turn the page

The Berthold red box appears in minia-ture on each inside page of the "Bert-hold zeigt Bild + Farbe" brochure

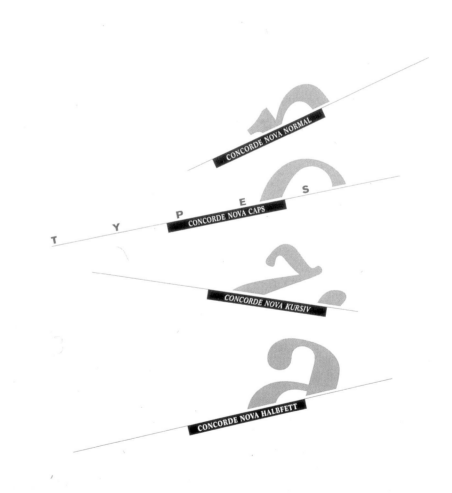

Brochure for the Berthold typeface Concorde Nova

SYNTHESIS

Inside front cover page introducing the Daily News typeface in various weights indicating the effects that can be produced with it

the starting point was the red square of the long-standing Berthold identity. MetaDesign added related design elements—a red bar to flag company products and services and additional red decorative elements for use on typeface brochures and other printed material. One of the company's core modern typefaces was selected as its house typeface. MetaDesign's creative strategy combines discipline in typography and in the identity elements with greater freedom in layout. This is seen to best effect in booklets designed to present specimens of the Berthold typefaces.

A LARGE, DIVERSIFIED INTERNATIONAL CORPORATION

Client:
Bowater plc, London, Great Britain

Corporate identity and design:
The Partners, London, Great Britain

Year:
1989

to assimilate under one identity the activities of a very large international corporation that has diversified from its original focal business while retaining the names of group member companies

The blue typography looks elegant
against the white facade of Bowater's
offices

The Partners' adoption of a bow-plus-water theme unwittingly echoes an earlier logotype

Bowater's previous logotype attempted to depict at least one of the company's activities in the abstract vocabulary of the time

t he devising and introduction of a new corporate identity for large international companies with many diversified interests raises problems quite different from those that confront consumer goods manufacturers and utilities that have a high public profile. These companies are often practically unknown to most people; it is often unclear what they make; they can support many seemingly unrelated activities. In these cases, a *new identity serves to send signals not to the public but to companies that belong to, trade with, or might be acquired by the group.*

Bowater was established in 1870 as a paper broker. It moved quickly into manufacturing to become one of the largest newsprint companies will mills in the United States, Australia and elsewhere in addition to its base in Britain. With paper subject to the price fluctuation of all commodities, Bowater sought to diversify during the 1960s, first into related activities—packaging, paper products etc—and later into other fields entirely such as freight, engineering and insurance.

In 1984, the highly successful American operation Bowater Inc. split off from the parent company. The British company Bowater Industries meanwhile suffered from poor management that led in due course to a buy-out. In 1987, the company was restructured under new senior management.

One legacy of the loss of the American Bowater was the loss also of the company logotype—a 1950s design with an archer's bow against a background of rippling water —as part of the sale agreement. Its replacement was a rather spiritless—and soon disliked—logotype in which the initial B was reversed out of a perspectival blue box.

A three-colour version of the final design would have given additional emphasis to the bow and water elements but was too expensive

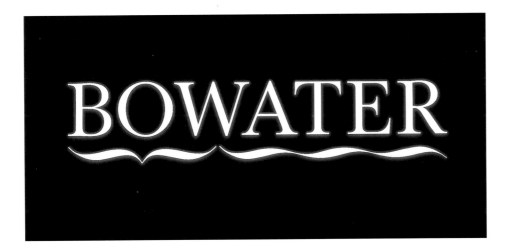

Bird stipulated his choice of a classical typeface, "preferably Baskerville", so there was little need for deliberation here

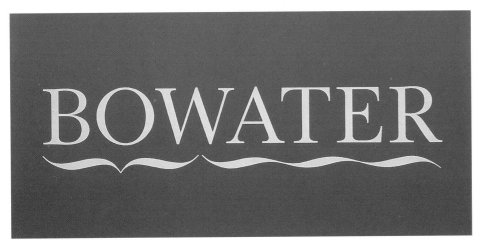

The basic design for the Bowater logotype finally chosen for reproduction in one colour only, white on blue or blue on white

The 1989 Annual Report celebrated one aspect of Bowater's diverse activities by its use of a cardboard pack

A number of variations on the theme were explored such as this transformation of the initial **B** into a bow

The superscript bow spells out the visual pun clearly and solves the problem of the **W** that overlaps both **BOW** and **WATER** elements

A few quite different corporate identity proposals, such as the creation of this flag, were quickly discarded

BRITISH VISUAL HUMOUR

Bob Bird, Bowater's director of group public relations, assumed responsibility for introducing a new corporate identity following the management buy-out. Having worked with The Partners at a previous company, he had no hesitation in commissioning them once again.

The Partners is modelled on the successful international design consultancy, Pentagram. Five designers head the company and also manage their own projects and project teams. Clients work directly with the designers rather than through project managers or account directors, a method well suited to Bird who has his own ideas about design. Aziz Cami was the partner in charge of the Bowater project.

All parties agreed the old B in a box had to go. Its anonymous abstract quality was inappropriate but Bird also ruled out any superficially "friendly" pictorial device.

"I'm against logos in principle. Many are not self-evident," he complains.

Bird admits a certain fondness for the old Bowater logotype, however, but summoned the strength not to go for the nostalgic option, instead favouring a typographic treatment.

"When you're talking about industrial companies, their name is their brand. If possible, you should utilise the company name as your logo form."

It was part of Bird's brief that The Partners make use of the company name and keep to a minimum the number of additional elements. Unusually for a client, Bird also specified that he wanted the name in a serif typeface, "preferably Baskerville". This he felt, would reflect the fact that the company was long-established and had an involvement in printing. Knowing The Partners as he does, Bird had no hesitancy in expressing his wishes, knowing too that The Partners would have told him his notions were wrong-headed if it were the case.

Brief consideration was given to graphic ideas that would describe the activities of Bowater companies, but these activities were so varied that the idea was soon dropped. The Partners settled on the bow-plus-water motif as something that would not overwhelm the Bowater and

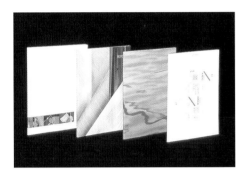

other group company names. In fact, they decided, it should literally underline them. The bow-plus-water passed the test of any good identity in that it could not easily apply to any other company. As a graphic pun on the words of the company name, it can be interpreted as a typically British piece of design.

The designers did look at a number of ways of representing the bow and the water. They wanted to employ a three-colour logotype, black for the typography, a golden bow and blue waves. Economic and practical arguments reduced this to just a vivid blue and white.

The Partners have produced the Annual Report for Bowater for each year since they were first commissioned

Inside, the annual reports are distinguished by their clear layout and high quality print and photography

The beauty of the **Bowater** underlining motif is that it works with a range of company names that are members of the Bowater Group

Bowater signage displays the logotype in a direct manner with liberal additions of the corporate blue colour

COMPUTERS AND TYPOGRAPHY

Macintosh computer technology has greatly facilitated the proportioning of the bow-plus-water underlining in cases of different company names. The procedure for producing each individual logotype has five stages: 1 the appropriate company name is computer typeset, then letterspaced by eye in the modified Baskerville Bowater alphabet; 2 the appropriate word is selected for underlining— usually the first word but the second if this is more significant; 3 the span of the bow under the first letters of the selected word is then chosen according to the point size of the lettering; 4 then the number of waves is calculated that most nearly brings the underlining to the end of the word; 5 finally, the wavelength of this part is compressed or stretched slightly for an exact fit. *Traditionally, all this would have had to be manually calculated and drawn. On the Macintosh, it takes only a few hours to create each symbol.*
The bow lies under the first two letters and part of the third. The system works well, but there is the occasional compromise. In the case of DRG Packaging, for example, the bow-plus-water underlines the word "packaging" and not the more significant "DRG", which is too short.
The beauty of the system is that it applies not only under the word Bowater but under other names which then acquire a hint of their Bowater parentage. In the US, for example, where it is no longer possible to use the Bowater name, the bow-plus-water underlining of the American company, which is in fact called Rexham Industrial, signals its affiliation to the British Bowater. This strategy honours the value of existing names.

"We strongly believe that a lot of the companies that we've inherited or acquired have very strong names within their industries," says Bird.

The aim of the new identity, says Shaun Dew of The Partners, was to do little more than to imply a largely autonomous subsidiary company's membership of the group. This preserves traditional names and ensures continued industry recognition for the subsidiary but there is a more brutal reason for taking this course. It can also be easier to buy and sell

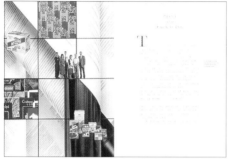

The 1990 Annual Report. All reports are now printed by a Bowater company, which was not necessarily the case formerly

group companies if they retain their historic names. Since the 1987 re-structuring there has been considerable buying and selling of companies as Bowater has sought to refocus its activities more on its core businesses. This new management strategy has had a strikingly beneficial effect on the company figures, even during hard economic times.

SPREADSHEETS IN PLACE OF MANUALS

The simplicity of the new corporate identity based on one typeface and one colour allowed The Partners to do away with the usual heavy identity implementation manual. Instead, the company was able to compress the necessary instructions into three folders. One introduces the logotype and the Bowater alphabet and shows their use on stationery and signage. The two others deal with implementation of the corporate identity on vehicles of various sorts. The same information was also printed on punched paper that could be inserted into a Filofax.
The leaflets are admirable in their simplicity. The general document,

"Our corporate identity", contains a cover introduction from Bowater's chief executive who describes the new design as "Open... taut... imaginative". The inside of the brochure explains the rationale for the Basker-ville house typeface and for the underlining, showing it with a variety of company names. A reproduction of a typed letter gives secretarial instructions on how to type letters to the correct format. The final tableau depicts Bowater signs, buildings and vehicles in their new livery and ends with a simple instruction: "The key to the success of our new corporate identity lies in presenting a unified and consistent front at literally every internal and external level. Please consult the Group Public Relations Department [ie. Bird] for advice and assistance before implementation." The vehicles brochures go into slightly more detail, for example specifying type sizes for lettering for decals or screenprints. This information is sufficient for member companies to prepare their own artwork, but they have the alternative option once again of referring to Bird for this work.
There was also a philosophical

The bow and water made a subtle appearance on the cover of the 1991 Annual Report which was packaged in a Bowater company bag

The cover of the 1992 Annual Report celebrates another Bowater activity with a die-cut of a pharmaceutical package used decoratively

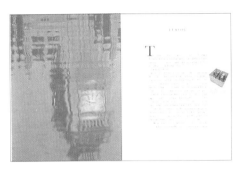

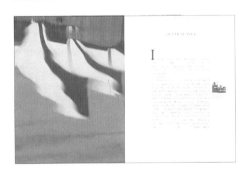

Reflections in water form a running theme for photography throughout the 1991 Annual Report

dimension to the decision to devise a more compact and usable format than the conventional unwieldy identity manual. This demanded recognition of the fact that problems will arise during the course of implementing the new identity no matter how comprehensive a manual might be produced. Rather than seek to produce the ultimate manual in an attempt to anticipate every difficulty, it was deemed better to acknowledge this fact and instead to involve the designers closely during implementation to correct errors and select the best option where there is a choice.

The new identity was introduced very gradually for economic reasons. *A company with a high consumer profile usually finds it beneficial to appear with its new image in one dramatic overnight move. An industrial company has the luxury of moving more gradually, making the change as need arises, thus incurring less additional expenditure.* The Bowater identity was introduced to the group's companies in the annual report, before being phased in over about a year.

Some groups reacted very positively to the new identity, rather like orphans that had found a parent. Many

of them began to ask to use the new identity ahead of the official time, when they were next reordering stationery, when their transport fleet needed a facelift, or when their buildings were to be refurbished.

Some groups were more resistant, especially those with a pre-existing logotype of their own. They were won round by being allowed to continue to use an old symbol as well as the type-based new identity. But one or two companies continue to fight a rearguard action.

> *"We've controlled the use of [old symbols] and tried to make them secondary to the company name—with varying degrees of success," admits Bird.*

Bowater's group companies are largely autonomous so maintaining control of the corporate identity is critical. Early on, there were some alarming interpretations of the bow-plus-water theme. (Surprisingly perhaps, the worst offenders were print companies!) Now, all original artwork, whether generated by The Partners or by Bowater companies, comes to Bird's department for approval— a temporary measure until the rules are sufficiently well understood that

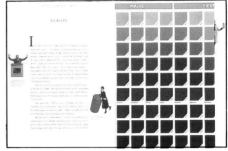

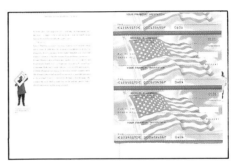

authorising artwork can be delegated. On occasion, however, thanks to the simplicity of typography and the single identity colour, it is possible to create artwork for specific projects that displays considerable creative freedom. Since 1988, Bowater's annual reports, for example, have been designed by The Partners to celebrate different aspects of Bowater's activities. High quality photography is used to highlight Bowater's paper and printing capabilities, for example. The 1992 report went a stage further, with a pharmaceutical cardboard box printed and cut into the cover.

The Partners fantasise that the bow and water motifs could be used in more varied, even humorous, ways, for signage and even furniture. Bird is more worried about the loss of control that would surely follow. Believing that design should lead by example, he finds it wrong as well as impractical with so many member companies to impose a will. But he adds: "We do stamp on anything truly horrendous." Bird has set his sights high. His wish is to do nothing less than engender a design-aware corporate culture at Bowater. He accepts that the process will probably take six to ten years.

The clarity of layout which The Partners established for their 1989 Report continues in the 1992 Report

Vehicle livery spread sheets produced by The Partners replace the traditional heavy corporate identity manual

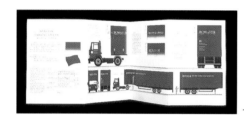

SYNTHESIS

the Partners rejected a modification of the old logo in favour of a new motif that would work with all member company names. The motif is an underlining made up of a bow shape and water ripples in a verbal-visual pun that is typical of British design. The underlining thus hints at the name of the parent company but does not allow it to obstruct the name of the subsidiary. The new identity has the virtue of flexibility, allowing Bowater's in-house designers to work with it in a variety of ways appropriate to new applications.

BT: PRIVATISED BRITISH NATIONAL TELEPHONE SERVICE

Client:
BT plc, London, Great Britain

Corporate identity and design:
Wolff Olins, London, Great Britain

Year:
1989-1991

to erase memories of British Telecom as an unpopular public service provider; to express its ambition to expand aggressively into new markets at home and abroad

Wolff Olins's proposed design for satellite dishes at Goonhilly show the cropped use of the identity symbol

The **BT** identity combines a symbol in human form representing the acts of communication alongside specially drawn lettering

The adhesive film used to apply the corporate symbol to vehicles is reflective providing high visibility at night

When, once in every quarter, Britain's major telephone service provider BT announces its profit figures, it is simply doing what every other private company must do. And yet when BT does this, it becomes the stuff of newspaper headlines. BT's quarterly profits are in the hundreds of millions of pounds. Its annual profit has topped £2 billion. The reaction of the press is to convert these figures into profit earnings per second, to report that, in the last quarter, BT made £90 per second, for example.

This treatment tells us two things. The first is simply that BT is a very large company indeed. The second is that something about BT's present practice or past history has occasioned a widespread resentment of its commercial success among the British people.

BT's guilty secret is that it was formerly the public sector telephone utility, British Telecom. Now privatised, though still largely a monopoly service provider in Britain, BT is indeed a large company, although in its new guise it is rapidly slimming down. At the time of its privatisation, it employed nearly a quarter of a million people. It has 88,000 telephone boxes, and thousands of buildings and vehicles.

Upon privatisation, in 1988, British Telecom gained a new head of design, Tony Key. One of his first actions was to undertake a thorough review of the existing corporate identity, produced by Banks and Miles as recently as 1981.

Key invited six consultancies to pitch for the job, evaluating them not so much for their ability to produce a striking new logotype but for their understanding of BT's strategic aims. Wolff Olins won the commission because they demonstrated during the course of two presentations and two more general discussions their conviction that a change of visual identity should reflect real change within the management structure and in attitudes to customer service. Only then would a new corporate identity be appropriate to give expression to the new ethos.

The new telephone books take a strong marketing stance in place of previous attempts at art patronage

Corporate identity entails more than new logotypes. Clearer bills, designed by **Siegel and Gale**, make a real difference to **BT** customers

MORE THAN A VISUAL MAKE-OVER

Certainly in Britain, and probably in Europe too where its clients include the Dutch chemicals manufacturer, Akzo, and the Spanish oil company, Repsol, no consultancy has done more to inculcate the notion that the practice of corporate identity involves more than just a visual image make-over. Change should cover everything from how the employees drive company vans to how they write letters to customers. Before its new identity was introduced, the future BT had introduced longer customer service office hours, provided easier access for people with questions about their telephone bills or additional BT services, and instructed employees to give their name as a contact when answering customers' calls. Whereas once many were vandalised or broken, the vast majority of public telephone boxes are now kept in working order. As Tony Key puts it:

"When you decide to change an identity, you change the culture of the company. The identity is to signify the change."

Telecommunications is a fast-changing field, both in the technology that is used to provide communications services and in the nature of service providers themselves, as national public monopolies once proud, later haughty and out of touch with the public that is their "market", and finally in demoralised decline. Wolff Olins chose a strong word to describe the general picture by stating:

"Telecom companies are abjuring their historical origins as publicly regulated utilities. But telecom companies have a traditional appearance and pattern of behaviour which derives from these origins. All over the world they look and feel like public sector institutions. BT is one of the first of the major telecoms to see and understand that the traditional mould in which the public utility telecom operates is no longer appropriate."

No one was surprised when research revealed that British Telecom was seen as cold, bureaucratic and unhelpful. Its managers wanted it to be seen by customers, including those in the international telecommunications market as well as domestic users, as an able global player, profit-oriented and efficient, fit to

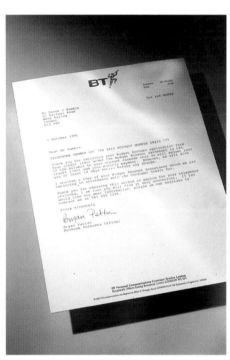

Wolff Olins's work involved not just the creation of a new letterhead but also advice on clear writing and layout

In some lights, the **BT** symbol almost disappears against the distinctive pale grey livery of the company's vehicles

The BT symbol is affixed to the atrium wall of the company's London headquarters building

stand alongside such American giants as IBM and AT&T. At the same time, it wanted to achieve the apparently contradictory aim of appearing warmer and friendlier.

The brief to Wolff Olins gave full leeway to recommend that BT abjure its past, if necessary dropping not only the old visual identity but also the name. As Wally Olins explains, in a case such as this, it was necessary to use all available tools in effect to re–train people who had spent their working lives in a atmosphere where

"the entrepreneurial instinct is almost crushed".

A six-month analysis of British Telecom's position revealed that if it was serious about achieving its aims, then it would have to change more drastically than it had imagined. What was wrong was not so much the scale of change envisaged, but the snail's pace at which the change was being made. Following a presentation by Wolff Olins to the British Telecom board, the company instigated Project Sovereign, dedicated to driving through all the necessary changes to the corporate culture and practice in a co-ordinated fashion.

TECHNOCRATIC CLICHÉS

British Telecom had pressing visible reasons to change in addition to finding a means of expression for its new privatised persona. The Banks and Miles symbol was a letter T in a circle with an embellishment of Morse-Code-like dots and dashes. Since its introduction, other national telephone companies, such as Spain's Telefónica and Hong Kong Telecom, had adopted similar visual vocabulary. *If British Telecom was to make headway in new markets, it would have to differentiate itself once again.*

Wally Olins terms this process a search for a new visual generic. Many avenues were pursued in the search for a name and a mark that would attain this status. In the end, the designers were not able to register a satisfactory name within the time available. The use of BT, the initials of the old name, was an acceptable fall-back position.

The new name provides a link with the past (many British people abbreviated British Telecom to "BT"), but it is no longer explicitly either "British" or a "Telecom" company. It was

British Telecom's old identity was inconsistent in its scaling of the two title words. Elsewhere, the T-in-a-circle motif had become tired

important to banish the "British" to destroy the idea that BT operated from a hub exclusively in Britain. Equally, the word "Telecom" serves no positive purpose. To its users, a telephone service provides a means to communicate with other people. The feeling of being at the frontiers of technology, portrayed in waveform curves or satellite silhouettes and the gratuitous use of high-tech jargon, is largely irrelevant. If one thing was known in advance about the company's new name, it was that it would not involve prefixes and suffixes such as Tele- or -com.

> "We didn't want to be seen as a hard high-tech company. We wanted to be high-tech but warm and friendly," says Key, adding: "I wasn't optimistic that we would achieve both."

(It is interesting to note that BT's logic is not shared by France Telecom whose new corporate identity by Landor Associates, announced at the end of 1992, chooses to retain a reference to both nationality and tele-communication.)
So much for what had to go. What did Wolff Olins put in its place? Olins's aim was to introduce a visual

Before the new identity was introduced, telephone books had covers with illustrations of local scenes, some by prominent artists

The BT Tower bears a large, illuminated symbol, but many Londoners continue to refer to the building fondly as the "Post Office Tower"

The bright yellow of the old vans conveyed a strong—and undesirable—sense of a public utility rather than an efficient company

The traditional elegance of BT's body typeface produces clear signs for BT buildings

idea to suggest, above all, that this telecommunications company would be different from any other such company with which the market might be familiar. Armed with one more reason to throw out the technological clichés, *Olins turned instead to what he calls a "universally comprehensible symbolism" that could transcend changes in technology and fashion alike,* renewing the established practice of drawing upon sources in mythology, such as the messenger god Mercury (ironically the name of BT's principal rival in Britain). The resulting visual mark is a human figure performing the two key acts of communication—broadcasting with pipes held to mouth and listening with hand cupped to ear. As one BT employee told Britain's *Design Magazine,*

"there's never been a nasty piper".

Wolff Olins has done much the same in the past for Akzo, whose symbol appropriates a human figure with arms outstretched as a system of proportion pertaining to both scientific and artistic life, and for the Prudential Insurance Company for which the figure of Prudence, one of the seven Virtues, was the source image.

The foyer at **BT** Centre designed by Imagination. Internal improvements are important in raising staff morale

Accompanying the figure are the letters BT drawn in a rather un-British custom typeface whose design was determined by what would look right alongside the graphics. Because of the ubiquitous nature of BT in Britain, the human figure has been used separately from the letters in some cases and has been cropped in different ways in different circumstances. It appears at its best in frosted glass on telephone boxes and as reflective panels on vans that shine when caught in car headlamps.

Olins and client director Valerie Allam both look forward to seeing the visual elements of the identity used with greater freedom in future. With a designed lifetime of around 15 years, there is plenty of time to develop variations on the theme.

MASSIVE IMPLEMENTATION PROGRAMME

The more immediate issue was to direct the massive programme of implementation of the new identity. Long before implementation, BT and Wolff Olins set up a corporate identity steering group to direct the activities of 15 task forces, each one responsible for one area of activity affected by the new identity introduction. These groups covered obvious categories of implementation such as vehicles, telephone boxes, buildings, signage, stationery, printed matter, BT retail sites, staff clothing and so on, but also task forces dealing with intellectual property issues and other less visible but no less important concerns. The fruit of their deliberations lies in the 30 or so corporate identity manuals that will eventually be produced. A single manual was out of the question on such a complex project. Instead, individual editions covering each aspect of the identity implementation are printed in suitable numbers for the people who need to know and in an appropriate medium for them to make the best use of them

BT's new corporate identity programme includes the introduction of new telephone booths, designed by BIB Design

BT, Privatised British national telephone service

The corporate image is particularly important in **BT** shops, one of the few places where the public directly encounters **BT**

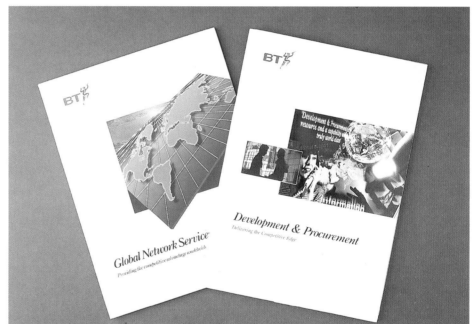

The interiors of the **BT** shops were designed by **Fitch RS** and further helped to banish the institutional feel of the former public utility

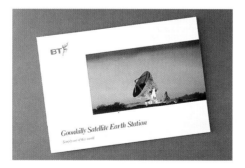

BT literature is created to a consistent style devised by **Wolff Olins** using colourful high-quality photography and illustration

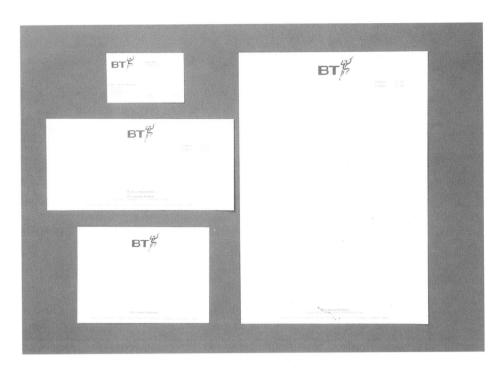

The **BT** identity symbol as applied to a range of stationery in a red and blue intended to be only faintly suggestive of **Britishness**

Additional copy is written on these envelopes in an elegant italic typeface and printed in the secondary corporate grey colour

BT's first Annual Review since the advent of the new corporate identity was designed by Michael Peters

New BT workwear is called "image clothing" rather than uniforms. The clothes were designed by Roland Klein

(for example, vehicle guidelines took the form of a laminated wall chart). BT organised seminars for relevant managers on manual usage and maintains a help desk for each of the subject headings covered by the task forces. If a manual does not prescribe a solution, Key's Corporate Design Unit devises a bespoke solution. This unit also exists to keep in line renegades who by accident or design produce work that does not conform to the manual guidelines.

"We don't stamp on their fingers, but we use the CDU to persuade them that the correct route is better," says Key.

For any properly conceived corporate identity, such persuasion should be a comparatively simple task.

Despite all the careful groundwork, the introduction of the new identity did not proceed quite to plan. Most of the creative work and implementation planning had been done far enough ahead of time that BT was able to sit on its new identity while it made further changes in management strategy. The company thought it then had the luxury of announcing the new identity at precisely the right moment, after sufficient change had been made that people would recognise the new mark as the expression

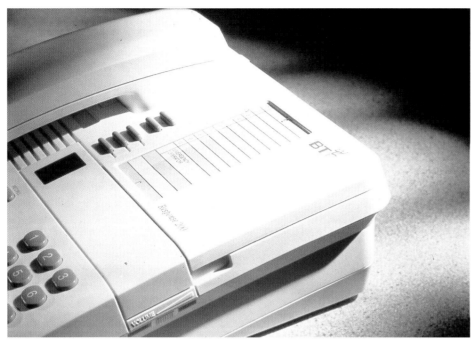

New products are designed to be consistent with the new design language and carry the identity symbol

of a new set of corporate values, but not so late that it would seem like an afterthought with no further real improvements to back it up.

However, the new logotype was leaked to the popular press. Uproar ensued centred on the alleged cost, with the usual confusion in the general press over the difference between design and other consultancy fees and (in this case very much larger) implementation costs. The professional design press also reacted critically but more on grounds of aesthetics than economics. Both groups largely overlooked the importance of underlying changes of which the new identity was just the visible expression.

While the cost and visual aspect of the new identity have undoubtedly been controversial, its implementation has proceeded to an enviably high standard and, given the scale of BT's operation, with considerable rapidity.

Recent research conducted in the wake of the launch controversy confirms that BT has indeed begun to achieve the seemingly impossible, to appear to its customers and potential customers as advanced and high-tech as well as friendly, accessible and human.

Existing booths carry the identity in frosted glass, but colours distinguishing cash and card phones clash with the identity colours

BT, Privatised British national telephone service

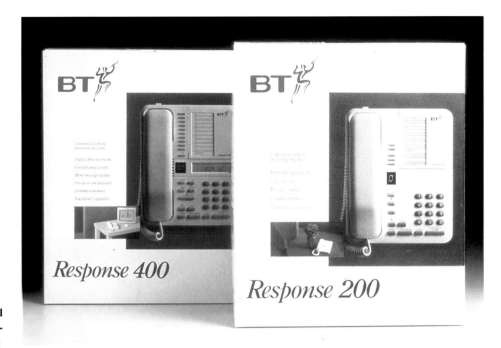

Product packaging by Coley Porter Bell makes prominent use of the new corporate identity to create striking branding

Basic elements page from the corporate identity guidelines

Many manuals describe the **BT** identity implementation, produced in quantities and media suited to the context in which they will be employed

The new corporate identity was announced in the internal newspaper, *BT Today*

SYNTHESIS

Wolff Olins did away with the old identity based on patterns of dots and dashes and a "T" in a circle. This had become a cliché widely imitated by European telephone companies. Avoiding a technocratic image entirely, the designers chose the fluid outline of a piper in red and blue accompanied by the letters BT in a custom typeface. The colours suggest the company's national origin. The initials and human motif are sufficiently distinct from European identities to provide competitive advantage and do not restrict BT to telecommunications activities.

A NEW IDENTITY FOR THE ARMED FORCES

Client:
Délégation Générale pour l'Armement, Paris, France

Corporate identity and design:
Desgrippes et Associés, Paris, France

Year:
1990

to create an accessible new identity that would heighten public awareness of a little known government agency and honour the federal nature of the organisation's various activities

The **DGA** symbol adorns this vessel of the **Direction des Constructions Navales**, but its style clashes with the logotype of this organisation

The **DGA** has embossed a range of attractive objects with the new identity as gifts for customers and potential customers

Exhibitions are a point of high public visibility for the DGA and an attractive exhibition stand is especially important

Desgrippes' corporate identity gives the DGA's hard-edged old arrowhead symbol a softer, contemporary treatment

many democracies around the world are making efforts such that their local and national government agencies and bureaucracies can respond better—or, at least, appear to respond better—to citizens' needs. These changes may be substantial or merely cosmetic, but in both cases corporate identity and design have made—and will undoubtedly continue to make—key contributions to the phenomenon. This policy has perhaps been pursued most enthusiastically in France, where it seems that every government office, cultural institution, *département*, city and town has at least a slick new logotype if not a full-blown corporate identity programme.

This widespread tendency has even reached as far as the Délégation Générale pour l'Armement, an agency of the French ministry of defence that is responsible for procurement and research for the armed forces. With a presumably secretive role and low public profile, such an organisation seemingly has little need of a professional or fashionable corporate identity.

Yet even an organisation such as this which is no corporation in the conventional sense can have valid reasons for implementing a "corporate" identity. In the case of the DGA, the reasons were both structural and emotional. The DGA had recently been reorganised and wished to convey the sense of the reorganisation by means of a new identity. The reorganisation involved an increase in central control in an attempt to draw together branches of the agency whose roots were spread among the various independent armed services. This shift of emphasis had two aims. The first was to cut costs, but the second and more interesting was to attempt to engender a common spirit—a sense of identity—among DGA staff.

Furthermore, the DGA's old identity was an austere arrowhead symbol created by the organisation itself rather than by a design consultancy. Hovering over an outline map of France, its crystalline shape looked rather like an alien spaceship. While this was one step removed from the authoritarian pseudo-heraldic motifs used by agencies of any number of governments, it was somewhat lacking in humanity. "We had an image which was too much industrial, too

technical and too aggressive," says Patrick Lamarque, the DGA's head of communication services. There was a marked disparity between the traditionalism of this symbol and the modernity of, for example, the scientific research that DGA was undertaking.

STRUCTURAL SIMILARITIES

Five design companies (all French in line with government strictures for such work) were invited to pitch for the project. The pitch was won by Desgrippes et Associés, an international design agency and part of the Desgrippes Cato Gobé group. Lamarque comments:

Examples of stationery: various notepad sheets, an envelope, letterhead and continuation sheet, dispatch note

> *"They were the closest to us. They were of the same mind. They understood the problem very well and found a very interesting creative method. The question of quality and the capability to organise a large and complex system was especially important."*

The DGA has 14 divisions and more than 50 production centres located around the country. Lamarque was impressed by Desgrippes' previous

A book of standards describes the implementation of the new identity in the federalised structure of the DGA offices

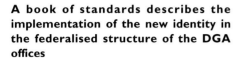

The cover of a brochure giving a brief description of the DGA logotype system shows a fragment of the symbol in a grey tint

work for Credit Agricole, a prominent national federation of banks structured quite like the DGA.

> "We found what they had done before for Credit Agricole was a good system, well executed and well organised. Our problem was very similar."

The style of Desgrippes' work evident in the Credit Agricole corporate identity also suggested that the design firm could satisfy Lamarque's demand for a less hostile image. The logotype that Desgrippes' creative director, Alain Doré, devised is indeed more friendly and informal than its predecessor, although it still manages to convey the military essence of the DGA's *raison d'être*. The design company offers this analysis of the logotype: "A first line stroke, directed downwards, illustrates the mission of protection for which the DGA is responsible. The arrow takes support in order to stretch itself upwards in a dynamic spirit of progress and efficacy, recalling its function as architect and master of works in research programmes into new materials and defence. An arc draws the sketch of a protective shield. In its pictorial treatment, it symbolises

the human resources and intelligence of the institution. An orange dot resolves the graphical construction. With its round form and its colour, this enlivens the dull tonality of the 'Bleu de France' that dominates the emblem. Finally, 'DGA' becomes the name *en bloc*. Its well constructed and frank typography is that of a solid and powerful institution."

NEW IMAGES OF OFFICIALDOM

The style of the work is very like that of other public sector institutions in France, not least because some others among them have also turned to Desgrippes. The national Ministère de la Solidarité, de la Santé et de la Protection Sociale, for example, employs a similarly paintbrushed look, but with the addition a human figure, arms outstretched against a rising sun, executed in warm, dominant colours. *Such figurative treatments are the very opposite of conventional images of officialdom.* In the case of the ministry of health, Desgrippes went still further, adding the slogan "chacun c'est moi" (which it transla-

tes as: "Everybody is me") to express the ministry's human dimension.

"To conceive the graphic image of a ministry is one of the most ambitious projects that can be entrusted to design professionals," acknowledges Desgrippes.

There are good reasons for this phenomenon of design in the French public sector. Patrick Lamarque, who worked in association with the Prime Minister's office during the mid 1980s, explains:

"In the regions, it's a consequence of legislation on decentralisation. In the field of national administration, it is a new way of thinking through our relationship with the public—not as numbers but as clients."

It is clear that the ministry of health and social protection has very many "clients" among the public, but surely the DGA makes its business exclusively with the commercial sector and government. This is not how Lamarque sees it. Admittedly, the new DGA identity is intended largely for internal benefit, but it also has a valid external role.

Its internal role is to give visible expression to the agency's changing role and to

Facsimile message form showing the reproduction of the corporate identity symbol in black only

Small adhesive labels are printed for specific exhibitions and other venues

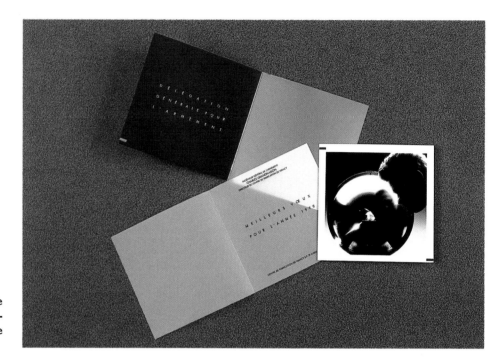

New Year greetings card adopts some of the colours and themes of the corporate identity for use in a more oblique way

Lapel badges for men and women DGA personnel enhance the appearance of professionalism for customers and the French public

raise morale and provide a flag for DGA staff to rally round. The logotype was announced to all DGA personnel by means of an eight-page folder, a complete presentation dossier, badges, a poster, and a six-minute introductory videotape packaged in boxes specially created for this purpose. All this material was also created by Desgrippes and appears to have produced the desired result.

"*[The new identity] is now very well known within the organisation, and people understood that we wanted to change. This was the main influence of this logo,*" says Lamarque.

The effort to create a "common spirit" was further enhanced by holding internal day conferences at which many DGA personnel, who normally work in the 50 regional centres, could gather to meet the organisation's top management.

EXTERNAL FUNCTION

The external function of the new identity is no less important although perhaps harder to build up for an organisation with very low public recognition. *Lamarque gives three reasons why it is important that the public be made aware of the DGA's existence: 1. The DGA need to recruit young engineers; 2. DGA plants and research centres are often the main employers in the towns where they are located and should therefore contribute to civic life; 3. In a democracy, there is a requirement to inform the public of what all government agencies are doing on behalf of their citizens.* Lamarque reports that the unveiling of the Desgrippes identity has raised public awareness from 21 per cent of people polled who had heard of the DGA in 1989, to 38 per cent in 1991, a year after the unveiling of the new identity.

In recruitment advertisements placed since 1990, the DGA has applied guidelines that include the use of the symbol together with the outline of a young professional male and the constant copy line: "J'ai choisi les responsabilités." A range of Frutiger typefaces is specified for these applications.

The DGA's visibility is increased still further by related material created by Desgrippes. This includes the design of exhibition stands and of a range of objects such as pens and calculators

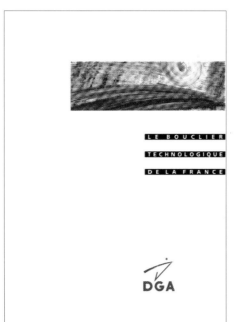

A catalogue of promotional objects also displays a fragment of the identity symbol in grey, but a different fragment from the brochure

A brochure describing the role of the DGA, produced in several languages, employs artwork that develops the symbol theme

marked with the DGA logotype intended as gifts for exhibition stand and agency site visitors and potential customers. DGA personnel wear lapel badges that bear the new symbol.

Like many contemporary corporate identities, Desgrippes' work for the DGA has been employed in a varied fashion, combining elements of the complete identity in different ways and in different styles. While a conventional corporate identity manual and a briefer graphic chart describe the "proper" implementation of the identity, these more creative uses are left to the designers' judgement. The covers of brochures that describe aspects of the DGA's activities, for example, have the symbol in its distinctive blue and orange stamped upon them, but they also use greatly magnified fragments of the symbol in a pale grey tint as a decorative element. Different brochures magnify different parts of the symbol.

A similar idea is used on one of the DGA's publications where the cover title uses the DGA letters in the typeface specified by Desgrippes together with a portion of the orange dot. The orange dot also serves as a

Company announcements are highly noticeable thanks to the prominent use of the red dot motif in the bottom corner

The Délégation's in-house magazine displays the DGA lettering prominently together with part of the identifying red dot in the title block

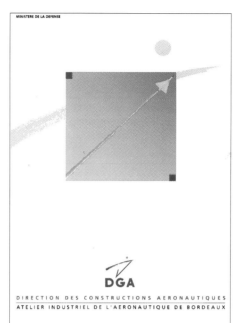

DGA identifier on company notices. Another range of brochures, describing the role of the DGA in several languages, adopts a quite different technique of varying the theme of the corporate identity by using a painter's striking reinterpretation of the blue and orange motifs. Seasonal greetings cards also treat the basic symbol as a starting point for the creation of a new graphic design.

The increasing reach of the DGA's blue and orange arrowhead marks the beginning of what Lamarque calls "a stylistic discourse". Change that has started with the introduction of the logotype onto company literature, gift objects and exhibitions is just the beginning.

"Now we must work hard in other fields of communication—internal communication systems, internal papers, magazines, information posters inside our plants and laboratories, electronic systems of communication, the buildings and so on. We are trying to give a general style to this organisation."

Brochures describing services of the DGA show the symbol used as a stamp rather than as part of a highly consistent identity scheme

SYNTHESIS

Material produced for the launch of the new corporate identity, an important occasion for DGA personnel

Under Desgrippes' guidance, the DGA discarded a previous symbol as too aggressive to fit in with its new values. The new logotype is an assemblage of sketch lines in French blue that communicate a modern, technological image while also expressing the contribution made by the organisation's human resources. Desgrippes created a video and additional literature for the launch of the new corporate identity to all DGA personnel and devised a range of image-oriented products for promotional purposes.

MUSIC AND BOOK PUBLISHERS

Client:
Faber and Faber, London, Great Britain

Corporate identity and design:
Pentagram, London, Great Britain

Year:
1981

to devise a logotype to reflect company changes and a more adventurous book list; to revive Faber's historical association with leading artists and illustrators in the design of book jackets and other material

A wide variety of artistic techniques and illustrative styles is used for Faber titles

The Faber logotype was used on book jackets before the house style was introduced that would give them common design elements

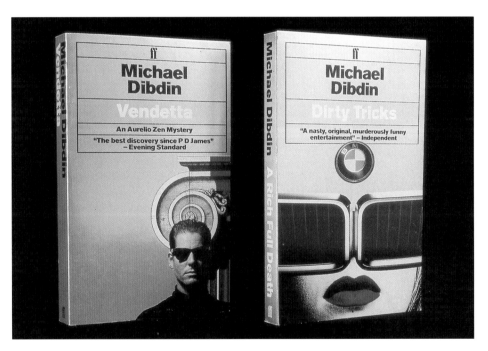

Bold Helvetica on silver combines the refinement of the Faber identity with the visual language of mass-market paperback design

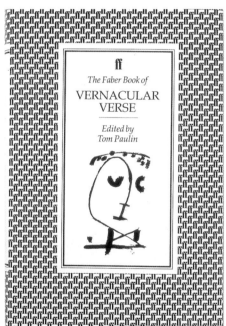

Faber's poetry titles have a family look with traditional overtones created by the repetition of the ff motif to form a patterned border

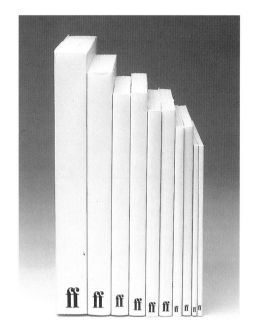

faber and faber

'Miroslav Holub is one of the half dozen most important poets writing anywhere'

Ted Hughes

A study to show how the logotype would appear on the spines of books of different sizes

McConnell's clarity and typographical refinement transfers well to posters promoting Faber authors

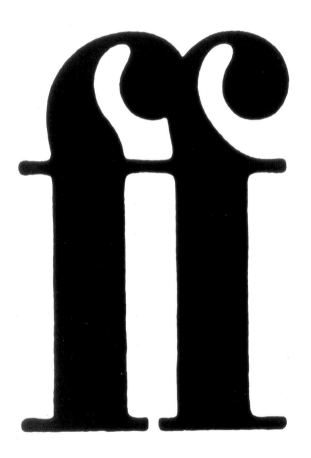

The publisher's full name, Faber and Faber, led to the decision to use the typographic ligature of the two letters ff for the main logotype

britain is known for its literary more than its visual culture. Occasionally, the two have come together with spectacular results. One such conjunction happened in the 1930s with the advent of the Penguin paperback. During the 1980s, the British publishing industry underwent a more complete revolution in design awareness, a revolution in which Faber and Faber played a leading part.

Faber and Faber claims to be the first British publisher to have taken charge of the design of its books, removing that responsibility from the printer. The German émigré Berthold Wolpe developed the Faber style through the 1940s, 1950s and 1960s, and later the company's in-house design department continued to employ what they thought of as the Wolpe style.

When Matthew Evans became chairman of Faber and Faber at the beginning of the 1980s, he quickly saw the problem. Faber and Faber was losing touch with its heritage of design excellence. After two abortive attempts—one from in-house designers, one from a design consultancy—to redeem the situation,

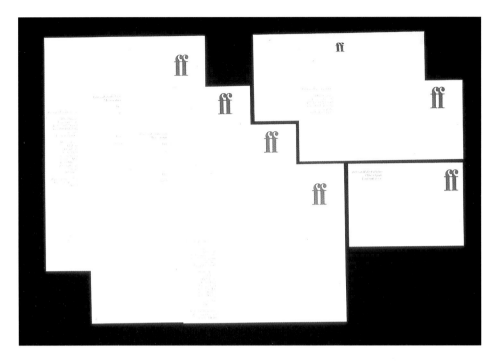

The Faber logotype on company stationery. The stark black-on-white treatment is a reminder of the printing process

The Faber Music logotype appears on
stationery in a similar manner to the
literature logotype

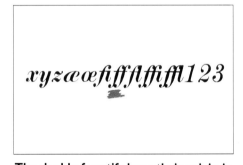

The double-f motifs have their origin in
printers' ligatures for setting characters
that would otherwise overlap when placed side by side

Evans's acquaintanceship with Ken-
neth Grange, the industrial design
partner of the London consultancy
Pentagram, led him to appoint one of
the group's graphic design partners,
John McConnell, to devise and imple-
ment a new corporate identity and
book jacket house style.

Surprisingly, perhaps, for one of the
top ten design consultancies in the
world (measured by fee income),
Pentagram picks up much of its business by word of mouth. Unlike some
competitors, it has weathered the
rapacious 1980s, the "designer decade", and is now well placed to restate
the case that success for a consultancy need not come at the expense
of creativity.

Evidence for this lies in Pentagram's
readiness to serve commercial clients
and do "pro bono" work side by side
without making value judgements
about either. For Pentagram, Faber
and Faber lay somewhere between
the two.

*"If they had charged us what they charge
their commercial clients we'd never have
been able to afford them," says Evans.
"They claim they've always run the
account at a loss."*

The parties do not discuss their full
consultancy fee basis, but readily
offer the information that each book
jacket must meet a budget of no
more than £500 for the illustration
and £100 for Pentagram. For Evans, it
is an additional benefit of working
with Pentagram that the consultancy
has access to a wide network of the
best illustrators.

*"They seem to be able to corral these
artists to do covers at well below the
market rate."*

*Yet more valuable is Pentagram's long-
standing policy that the client communi-
cates directly with the partner who is
actually doing the design work. The top-
level communication works to mutual
benefit. Evans is happy that, unprompt-
ed, Pentagram will draw attention to an
area where the publisher's presentation
may be flagging and suggest a change.*

*"It's a partnership with input and argu-
ment and debate coming from both sides
all the time. Many other design groups
would treat Faber and Faber as simply
another client."*

When used with some of the more austere illustrations, Faber covers resem-
ble those of famous French and German paperback publishers

Faber's film titles transform the title
box into a clapperboard, a joke that
works because the shapes and colours
blend well with the basic design

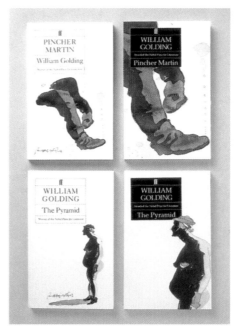

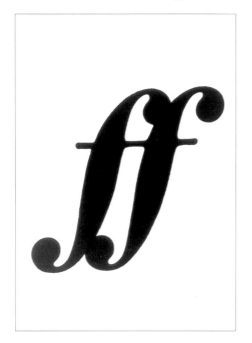

Following logically from the main
logotype, the symbol for Faber's music
publishing is the equivalent ligature
from musical notation

Pentagram partners also work together with each other more as a co-
operative than as a corporation.

*"Pentagram is purely a vehicle for individuals
to do their own thing," says McConnell. Each
partner is responsible for his or her own
staff, projects and profits. By operating as
lots of little businesses, McConnell adds, "we
do the same amount of design work as the
guy who runs a small business. The partner
runs his group as he wants to, and does as
much administration as ensures that he can
fulfil his projects and run his team."*

DOUBLE FF LIGATURE

McConnell chose a printer's double ff
ligature as the logotype, replacing or
for use in addition to the words Faber
and Faber. A particular elegance is the
parallel logotype for Faber's music
publishing activity, a similar ff ligature
in italics, the musical notation for *fort-
issimo.* The devices have that obvious
rightness of the best logotypes, and
yet they were far from popular when
first introduced. The sales staff
thought it a mistake to forgo any
opportunity to impress the company's
name in full. The fusty book trade
press found the new identity too vul-
gar. Anticipating some such opposi-
tion, the new identity was first imple-
mented in company stationery and
only gradually introduced for book jackets. *Pushed through with the full back-
ing of the Faber management, the new
look took about a year to win general
acceptance within the company as it gradually appeared on catalogues, point-of-
sale displays and other material before it
was seen on any book.*

To some extent, McConnell was using
these projects to test the water. The
introduction of a new corporate identity can involve as much personnel

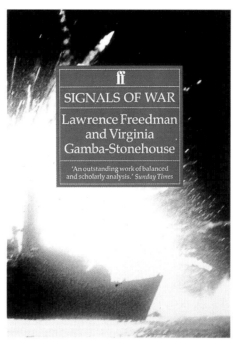

Long titles, subtitles, or complex and multiple authors can all be handled within the format of the title box with its flexible box heights

handling as design. McConnell enlisted one ally from the existing in-house design team, all the rest of whom opposed change, feeling (not without reason, as events turned out) that their jobs were threatened.

The ligatures were just a beginning. For the book jackets—the most visible expression of Faber and Faber's identity as well as the one required to make a commercial impact—McConnell had to develop both a design vocabulary and a system by which it could reliably be expressed on 230 new titles each year.

Faber's published plays are signified by a decorative frieze derived from theatre playbills

In the case of a prolific playwright, one particular colour scheme may be chosen to "brand" that author within the poetry series

While black was the agreed colour for most fiction title boxes, non-fiction took a variety of colours

New artwork is sometimes commissioned when a successful title is reprinted thus keeping an author's "Branding" up to date

A number of anthologies published by Faber make appropriate use of collage around a central title panel

CONTROL VERSUS FREEDOM

Faber and Faber's list breaks conveniently into several specialist areas. Jackets to plays, for example, sport a geometric design derived from traditional playbills. Poetry books use a "wallpaper" design that repeats the ff motif to produce a quite different traditional feel.

But for general fiction and non-fiction, there is a common system comprising a fine-ruled rectangular box that contains the ff ligature, a book's title and the name of its author. The type is in the same crisp serif face. This box is generally black, but this is not a rigid rule. Within fiction and non-fiction, there are also "sub-brands". A new list of mass-market fiction, the sort that sells well at airports, has a shiny silver box with bold Helvetica type.

Both McConnell and Evans talk about an ideal condition in which the Faber and Faber corporate identity could be employed with complete control. (McConnell admires the uncompromising pursuit of order of some continental paperback publishers, notably Germany's DTV; Evans eulogises about simplified design administra-

The title box, which started out as black only for fiction titles, has gradually assumed new colours to complement particular cover artwork

Medical titles were assigned a blue title box, but this is not a rigid rule. Some fiction titles also use blue

Title boxes appear either in the colour of the cover art background or in a complementary colour to highlight aspects of the artwork

The style of individual illustrators contrasts well with the refined typography within each book's title box

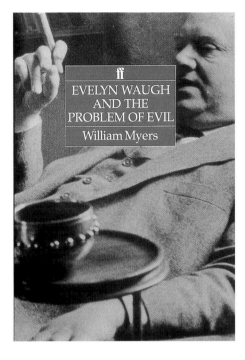

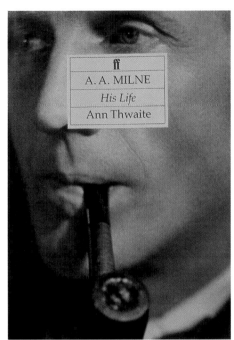

On occasion, it can be hard to position the title box over the chosen cover art. Careful positioning, however, renews focus on the photograph

McConnell chose the illustrators Huntley/Muir as appropriate for this collection of women's erotic literature

tion). In reality, matters are a little more complicated.

There is a certain conflict between the systematic and the impulsive. It can be unclear, for example, whether or not the use of a particular colour signifies anything. Medical titles are signified by a blue title box, for example, but fiction titles can also appear in blue—or red or yellow or white—for no better reason than that colour better complements the cover artwork. In a very few cases, the subversion goes rather further. A series of books on wines presents the title box as the label on the bottle in the cover photograph.

The publishing business is notorious for the vagueness with which it conducts its business, and Faber and Faber has no measure of the effectiveness of its identity and no proof that it has produced increased sales, although Evans does have strong circumstantial evidence for its success. It was introduced at a time when many British publishers were making efforts to smarten up the visual aspect of their product. At the same time, major book stores such as Dillons and Waterstone's were conspicuous by their interior design.

Evans says the two design trends are interconnected: well designed stores give more prominence to well designed books. "We get an enormous number of window displays and more covers facing out in book shops that we would not get otherwise."

Evans gives McConnell all credit for devising a working routine that ensures a high standard of book jackets is maintained. McConnell's masterstroke was to demand that, at the fortnightly meetings when cover design concepts are decided, each book's editor read out loud the brief for its cover. The result is that the editors think harder about what would be appropriate. In practical terms, it spares McConnell and his Pentagram assistants having to read each book. From this brief, McConnell assigns a designer or illustrator whose style is thought appropriate.

The illustration serves as the antidote to the rigidity of the cover design framework. After ten years, Faber and Faber's book jackets serve as a gallery of the best in contemporary illustration and effectively renew the publisher's commitment in this field. Past artists commissioned include McKnight Kauffer, Graham Sutherland,

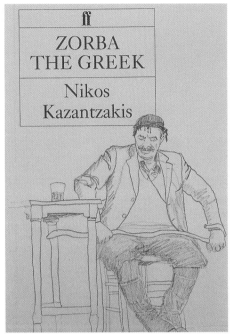

The pointillist style of Pierre le Tan's illustrations fits well with the closely observed narratives of author Garrison Keillor

The logic used for artwork is often intuitive and based on personal acquaintance. Here, McConnell simply selected a good Greek illustrator

John Piper, Eric Gill, Laszlo Moholy-Nagy. Today, the pointillist illustrations of Pierre le Tan have established a strong "brand identity" for the books of the American humorist Garrison Keillor. Huntley/Muir's painterly style enlivens a number of gay titles. In each case the illustrator's style and character are in some sense congruent with that of the author.

All art must work in conjunction with the cover title box. This can sometimes seem like an obstacle. At best, however, this constraint produces a tension between type and image. This is especially pronounced in some of the film titles whose covers display striking black-and-white photography.

ON THE COMPANY BOARD

McConnell has the ultimate responsibility for design decisions. On occasion, Faber's in-house design manager has co-ordinated a cover design without reference to Pentagram but this only happens when circumstances make it unavoidable. Evans is amazed—and relieved—that the regular commitment has held McConnell's interest for eight years—the more so since he doesn't read the books or come to Faber's literary parties. Although the regular meetings have proved educational to the point where McConnell admits that sales and management staff have an eye for an appropriate design, Evans knows that if book jacket design and corporate identity management were brought in-house, it would not only greatly increase workload, but also lead inexorably to a watered-down Pentagram style as it once led to a watered-down Wolpe style.

McConnell's contribution to Faber and Faber does not stop here. *He was made a board member of the company, not only to signal the continuing importance of design for the company, but also because his business experience*

A point-of-sale display carries the Faber logotype. In locations such as these the strong design house style is particularly eye-catching

Faber's semi-annual catalogue makes bold use of an illustration from one of the new titles of the season

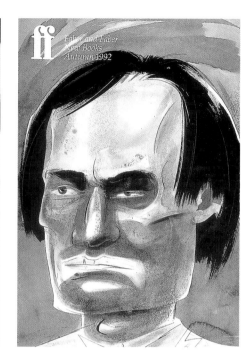

There is a conspicuous example of rule-breaking in a series of titles on wines where the sacrosanct title box becomes the "wine label"

at Pentagram can be brought to bear on the publisher's activities. There are direct parallels. McConnell's experience in the hard-headed world of fast-moving consumer goods with the British pharmacy chain, Boots, has led to point-of-sale innovations, for example.

But there is potential for the designer to bring far greater change. Pentagram's rule that each partner should function as a profit centre finds its parallel in the notion that each Faber book might be considered as a profit centre. It does not necessarily mean what authors and traditional publishers might fear—that each book must make a profit— merely that it should be known whether each book makes a profit or a loss and by how much. This knowledge, McConnell reasons, makes business planning simpler and brings loss-making books out of the closet. Once this confession is made, such books can be cause for pride rather than shame just as Pentagram's "pro bono" projects serve a cause with no pretence of making money. This proposal, radical by the standards of the publishing trade, illustrates the extent to which a good designer can redesign not just a company's image but also key aspects of its commercial conduct.

SYNTHESIS

A simple illustration forms the centre-piece of each poetry title, but the series style created by the "ff wallpaper" is what stands out most

Pentagram's contribution centred on a new logotype based on a printer's ligature formed by Faber and Faber's initial letters. A related ligature based on musical notation was employed for the company's music publishing activity. With its client, Pentagram plans and commissions book jacket designs from leading artists and illustrators. In conjunction with this artwork, the logotype identifies Faber as a leading publisher in both commercial and creative terms while the illustrations themselves allow the books to compete in the design-aware British book market.

NIPPON LIFE INSURANCE COMPANY

Client:
Nippon Life Insurance Company, Osaka, Japan

Corporate identity and design:
Chermayeff and Geismar, New York, USA

Year:
1987-1988

to give the world's second largest life insurance company a new image befitting its ambitions to diversify within the financial services market and to play a more active international role

New building signs employ Chermayeff and Geismar's symbol together with PAOS's vertical Japanese logotype

The corporate symbol makes a bold impact in the chaotic visual environment that is urban Japan

In addition to the interlocking squares motif, Nippon Life also used to employ its name in Japanese characters in a variety of formats

The logotype took a variety of appearances according to the nature of the building or context in which it was used

Nippon Life's old identity resembled many in Japan with their origins in heraldry but appeared archaic in the modern financial sector

the field of financial services represents one of the greatest market opportunities and one of the greatest challenges for the corporate identity specialist. It is an opportunity because recent deregulation and growth in both local and global competition have given financial services providers such as banks, building societies and insurance companies occasion to use design to differentiate themselves from their competitors. It is a challenge because *the ingrained conservatism of these companies very often means that, despite the fact that they have no tangible product to offer, they are often very slow to realise the importance design can have in defining their role and identity in the modern marketplace.*

Some of the largest financial services corporations have been among the first to make the change. The Nippon Life Insurance Company is a case in point. The largest life insurance company in Japan for the duration of the century, Nippon Life is fortunate to operate in a large country where life insurance is taken very seriously by its citizens. This makes it a giant by any standards. In 1987, as the brief for the new corporate identity was being pre-

pared, its assets stood at 15 trillion yen, and it stood poised to overtake the world's largest insurance company, the Prudential (which had also seen the importance of change to reflect a transformed marketplace and had adopted a new corporate identity, created by Wolff Olins, around this time).

Nippon Life, which in Japanese becomes the one word Nissei, has its headquarters in Osaka and maintains more than 120 offices throughout Japan as well as an overseas network of representative offices in major cities throughout the world. The company celebrated its centenary in 1989, and required its new corporate identity in time to mark this event, as well as to take account of sweeping social changes in Japan and market changes at home and abroad. The introduction of a new corporate symbol, logotype and design system was to presage more substantial changes in corporate practice.

One requirement was for a simple identity that could work flexibly, in colour or black-and-white and in horizontal or vertical formats

AMERICAN EXPERTISE

Like many Japanese corporations with an eye on export markets, Nippon Life turned its back on Japanese designers (many of whom are extremely talented in design terms but lack the track record so beloved of Japanese industry when it comes to the minutiae of corporate identity implementation) and looked to the corporate identity experts in the United States. Among the Japanese corporations to have trodden this path recently are Japan Airlines, Minolta and Sanyo who went respectively to Landor Associates, Saul Bass and Anspach Grossman & Portugal for their new identity designs. For its part, Nippon Life chose the New York consultancy, Chermayeff and Geismar.

The designers' first visit to learn about their client and its operating environment was not an inspiring experience. They found a harsh working regime in which a sales force entirely made up of women, many of whom bicycle long distances to get to work, is managed entirely by men. Few saleswomen last more than a year in the job.

The designers also learned that it is women who generally purchase insurance in Japan, a country where the great majority of people insure themselves as well as their possessions and even attributes such as their golf scores. Due to the rise in personal income that has come with Japan's post-war economic growth, uptake of these services has been such that more than 90 per cent of households participate in some form of life insurance plan.

While this behaviour underpinned Nippon Life's success, the company now wished to diversify into offering financial services other than insurance policies such as investment in securities and real estate. Indeed, shortly before the new identity was commissioned, Nippon Life acquired a share of the US securities company Shearson Lehman Brothers.

The background to the commission was stated in a report prepared by the client and the Japanese liaison consultancy, PAOS:

"Nippon Life must balance diversity against unity to keep its large organisation together and to provide the wide

The adoption of the anglicised Nissay name opened an avenue to English copy-lines making further use of the word "say"

A Nissay building in Nagoya shows the corporate symbol employed effectively without the use of the corporate red colour

Chermayeff and Geismar's model for the three-dimensional sculptural version of the symbol echoes some of the designers' previous well known work

The corporate symbol stands out clearly in newspaper advertisements providing a lead-in to the "Nissay says..." copy

variety of policies and services that the contemporary market requires. Nippon Life is viewed by industry watchers as the most untypical and innovative firm in the generally conservative Japanese life insurance industry. ... Nippon Life has seen its role as provider of security and well-being to the Japanese people. Its long-range strategy ... is to play an active international role as well. ... Its logo must therefore serve the company from Tokyo to Frankfurt, from Singapore to New York."

Market research studies found that the company name was well known but that the nature of its work was not. It was admired for its "corporate strength and reliability", its "cohesion and solidarity" and "warmth and approachability". But specific problems emerged in conflict with these generally positive attributes. Pushy sales staff gave the company a negative image. *Beneath the surface was the more intractable introspective nature of the company—something that it recognised would have to change in the liberalised, international competitive world of modern financial services competition.* In addition, there was no coherent vision of how Nippon Life should portray itself. Rather, each department had its own ideas.

PAOS concluded that Nippon Life should seek to retain its pre-eminent position in its field, but to present itself as more youthful, vigorous and friendly, regarding its vast human resource of 80,000 staff as "nextdoor neighbours to its customers".

Corporate Identity

Glass etching for doors illustrates the varied use of the Crystal symbol in different media

JAPANESE CHARACTER

Nippon Life's old corporate symbol was symptomatic of its hidebound ways. The two interlocked squares enclosing a Japanese character was typical of traditional marks in the country many of which (such as the well known and simple symbols for Mitsubishi and Sumitomo) have been passed on largely unaltered from their original use as family crests dating back in some cases to medieval times. As a symbol, it was elegant enough, but lacked individuality. Its archaic quality meant that, in the changed context of modern Japan, it looked more like the mark used on a cask of soy sauce than the emblem of a major international financial institution. Other marks and logotypes were equally undistinguished. To add insult to injury, the central character, "sei", which originally meant "life", had now come to be associated with another word meaning "draft (beer)". Before Chermayeff and Geismar were appointed, Nissei made the decision to anglicise its name to "Nissay". This move had a number of justifications. It made the company seem more international to the Japanese, but also

less foreign to potential customers abroad. The -say suffix had the added benefit, in English, of connoting an act of human communication.

The criteria for the new corporate symbol that was to accompany the new Nissay name were that it should be progressive, cosmopolitan and human in feeling. The designers had to balance internationalism with "Japaneseness".

"They were against being thought of as Japanese as they usually are in these situations," says Chermayeff. *"They reject their heritage as a stance. My own interpretation is that it's all very well to say this, but it is not sensible or feasible."*

In use, the symbol should be distinctive, easily recognised at a distance and easily reproduced in colour or black-and-white, positive or negative. In common with many modern corporate symbols, a requirement was laid down that the new mark should have the potential to be used in a variety of ways.

All 20 Nippon Life company directors attended a presentation at which three proposals devised by Chermayeff and Geismar were discussed in

The spirit of Chermayeff and Geismar's design is somewhat diluted in much of the company literature

日本生命保険相互会社

Nippon Life Insurance Company

The red diamond appears as a modest mark on company literature, but corporate colours and typefaces are not used throughout

considerable detail. The design which came to be known as the Nissay Century Crystal or Nissay Diamond was preferred.

Ivan Chermayeff and Tom Geismar provided the following interpretation of their "crystal":

"The Nissay symbol is to us a meeting of two worlds—the traditional and the modern, the classic square and the triangle are both used together to suggest the letter N of the new name—Nissay.

"The square symbolises the four directions of the compass (north, south, east and west), four elements of the universe (earth, fire, water and air) and the four seasons of the year (spring, summer, fall and winter).

"The symbol puts these meanings into balance. Within the square are the triangles—symbols of life, embodying the idea of the family—father, mother, child or the metaphysical idea of the body, spirit, soul. The triangle is also the triangle of divinity, of humanness and of nature."

In places, this text is an extreme example of the hokum that often accompanies a prospective new design. The intent is sincere—symbols should have meaning, and that

meaning should be made clear to the client—but the process has become something of a self-parody. Some of these meanings are legitimate but others are the product of spurious post-rationalisation.

HARMONY OF GEOMETRY

What Chermayeff and Geismar do not state is their achievement in designing a symbol that appears entirely modern and yet which also, thanks to its geometry, has some of the ineffable quality of traditional Japanese symbols. Simple rules of proportion govern the composition. If we assign an arbitrary length of two units to the sides of the red diamond, we find that the points of the N bisect each of the four edge lines of the diamond at its midpoint; that the vertical height of the N is the square root of two units; that the long and short diagonals of the N are respectively half the square root of five units and half a unit in length. The overall area of the symbol is four square units, while its component two red triangles each occupy half a square unit and its two remaining red quadri-

Rooftop placards display the corporate symbol in conjunction with English and Japanese logotypes in a variety of layouts

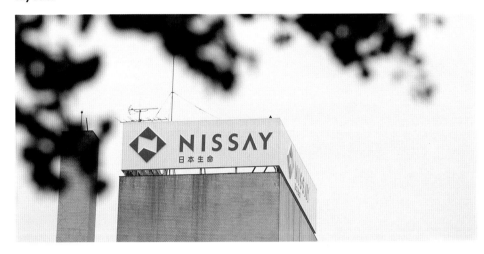

The sharpness of the Nissay lettering lends something of the quality of Japanese calligraphy to the logotype

The corporate symbol is displayed to good effect at a building entrance

The elegant geometry of Chermayeff and Geismar's design shows clearly on these introductory corporate folders

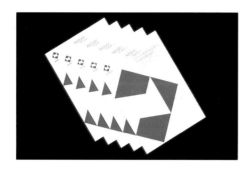

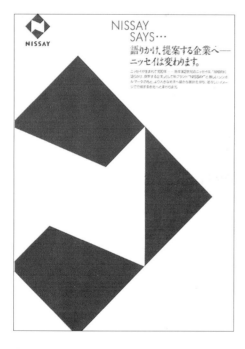

The origami-like nature of the red diamond is made more explicit when one corner of the symbol is folded around the spine of this folder

lateral shapes have areas of three-quarters of a square unit. The white area of the N itself is thus one and a half square units and three-fifths of the total red area. There are resonances with the proportions of the golden section in this geometric form. Furthermore, *it cannot be coincidental that the symbol looks like a piece of origami paper* with fold lines marked upon it.

Certainly, the Century Crystal is more distinctive than one of Chermayeff and Geismar's other proposals, which incorporates the Nissay N into a globe with diagonal hatched lines. The rationale for this scheme was that a circle symbolises eternity as well as internationalism and is a favoured shape on Japanese coats of arms as well as the national flag.

A vivid red was selected as the corporate colour for the Nissay diamond. This retains the equity of the old symbol and honours tradition in Japan where red is an auspicious colour, while the brightened colour gives a contemporary appearance.

For the Western Nissay logotype lettering, *Chermayeff and Geismar adopted what has become almost a cliché among Japanese firms seeking to strad-* dle Western and Japanese cultures of using Roman letters in a crisp sans serif face so that the sharp corners of certain letters echo the lines of Japanese calligraphy. Many Japanese consumer electronics companies have taken this road. In this case, Chermayeff and Geismar used a specially drawn Futura typeface in a warm grey and enhanced the effect for better recognition by customising the letters N, by adding points, and A, by removing its crossbar.

"As it is, it is a bridge of acceptability that has Japanese overtones," says Chermayeff. *"If you see it in London or New York without Japanese characters it doesn't immediately say Japanese to you."*

The lettering can be used centred below the N diamond or alongside it depending upon the demands of the application.

This was the extent of Chermayeff and Geismar's involvement. From here on, the Japanese agency PAOS co-ordinated implementation of the corporate identity and the production of a Japanese identity manual. Implementation was no small task for a corporation the size of Nippon Life but was carried out quickly in compa-

On such an object as a matchbox printed without any lettering, the Nippon Life symbol has an enigmatic, abstract quality

On printed matter, Chermayeff and Geismar's "Century Crystal" appears in various sizes

The single bold colour of the symbol appears rather like a stamp on printed matter such as company stationery

rison with design implementations at most companies of this scale. The unveiling of the new identity in most of Nissay's branches was followed up with a national advertising campaign. Reaction to the new identity both from personnel and from the Japanese public is reported to be positive, turning up such positive adjectives as "conspicuous", "memorable", "distinctive", "timely" and "unique".

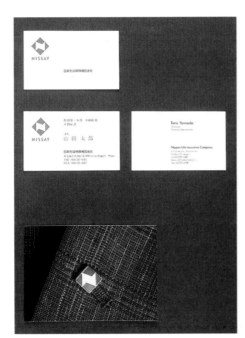

Prominently identified business cards and lapel pins create a strong corporate presence where Nippon Life staff interact with customers

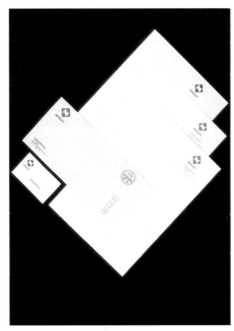

Stationery is printed in the corporate colours—warm grey and bright, almost fluorescent, red

Business cards constitute a major aspect of Nissay's public facade, so the symbol is more prominently displayed than in the past

Lapel pins act as a focus for company pride, helping to combat former negative customer reaction to encounters with pushy sales staff

Seen to best effect against an uninterrupted white background, the red diamond symbol and grey lettering have a sharp modern look

Nippon Life, known as Nissei in Japan, anglicised its name to Nissay which now appears alongside the corporate symbol in most cases

The word Nissay appears on all stationery emphasising the international nature of the company to the Japanese market

SYNTHESIS

Ease of recognition was a prime criterion for the new corporate identity allowing it to be used as a discreet colour element

Working through the offices of a design consultancy in Japan which was responsible for liaison with the client, Chermayeff and Geismar designed a bright new symbol, and an accompanying logotype and lettering, that conveyed the required sense of modernity and internationalism while still retaining links to the tradition of Japanese heraldic symbols and calligraphy. Chermayeff and Geismar developed the elements of the design and the system for their implementation which was then undertaken in conjunction with the local consultancy.

WRITING TECHNIQUES

Client:
Olivetti, Ivrea, Italy

Corporate identity and design:
Walter Ballmer at Olivetti

Year:
1970

to create a minimum logotype that grows out of previous logotypes to serve as a framework allowing for continued strong and individual creative expression in all areas of company design

**FRIENDLY
&
COMPATIBLE**

Some modern artwork has lost the playfulness of former eras, but the Olivetti logotype is placed consistently

THE PERSONAL COMPUTER FAMILY WITH EUROPEAN KNOW-HOW

olivetti

1976 Christmas advertising poster by Egidio Bonfante. The legend reads: "Bring me a portable"

The Olivetti signature as it appears on the M1 typewriter, the first Olivetti product

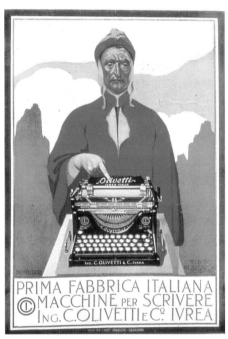

1912 poster by Teodoro Wolf-Ferrari shows Dante recommending the M1, Olivetti's first product

O livetti has nurtured an enviable reputation for the patronage of good design in all fields during the 85 years of its existence. So to single out "corporate identity design" from among Olivetti's areas of excellence is meaningless. It is only by examining the patronage of all the design professions by Olivetti—and indeed by examining that patronage in the far broader context of Italian culture as a whole—that a measure of the company's achievement may be gained.

Foreign observers seeking to examine the prominence given to design at Olivetti quickly light upon the importance of something vaguely termed "the Italian culture" in shaping the company's attitude. While it is virtually unavoidable that we should wonder at this, the scrutiny merely perplexes the Italians themselves, so deeply rooted is the culture in everyday matters of life and business.

It is this symbiosis of commercial and cultural priorities that gives much of Italian industry its confidence as it confronts ever more competitive markets. At Olivetti, it helps to explain how two of the world's best industrial designers, Ettore Sottsass Jr. and Mario Bellini, were "found" by Olivetti not when they were already running successful consultancies, but at the outset of their careers, based on sight—and comprehension of the merit—of early projects, or, more telling still, from having read their writings.

It is well known that IBM's Thomas J. Watson Jr. was influenced by Olivetti's outstanding design in the 1950s. But Adriano Olivetti, son of the company founder, Camillo, was much influenced by the United States, where he admired the latest advertising techniques and the new ideas about corporate image-building. Upon his return to Italy, he applied what he had seen but within the Italian context that presumed a greater cultural literacy.

Milton Glaser's 1970s posters often took their cue from classic fine art, another manifestation of Olivetti's cultural literacy

1920 poster by Pirovano advertising the M20 typewriter echoed the spirit of the Italian Futurist movement

1935 poster by X. Schawinsky shows the M1 typewriter with Camillo Olivetti's monogram initials I, C, O in line

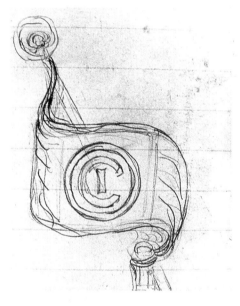

Sketch of the monogram for Ingegnere Camillo Olivetti that was the company symbol before it adopted a formal corporate identity

CULTURAL GAMES

Consider one of Olivetti's most famous products, the Valentine typewriter. Designed by Ettore Sottsass in the 1960s, this bright red portable signalled through its design its intention to break free of the conventional wisdom of how such things should look. This typewriter was recreational, even playful. Milton Glaser's posters advertising the product—impishly inserting it into details of classical paintings—developed the theme of playfulness.

The union of spirit between graphics and products is perhaps closest, however, with the earlier posters of Giovanni Pintori for the machines designed by Marcello Nizzoli. The Olivetti patronage is notable for these high points, but also for its continuity. Where other 20th-century patrons of design have experienced one period that surpassed others (for example, London Transport during the 1920s and 1930s), Olivetti has rarely slipped. As Renzo Zorzi, the company's consultant on cultural activities, writes in *Design Process Olivetti 1908-1983*, a work published by the company to celebrate 75 years of design leadership: *"There are times when product design takes first place, and others when architectural achievements are prominent, or when the company's relationship with its public is most strongly typified by its graphics work, ... But no strand is ever broken..."*

Olivetti's first typewriter went into production in 1911. Even with this first product, the M1, which well predated the emergence of a distinct profession of industrial design, Olivetti recognised that the aesthetics of the object were important. He also saw no distinction between excellence in three dimensions and excellence in two dimensions. Graphic design was the equal of product design from the beginning, seen in magnificent advertising posters, by Teodoro Wolf-Ferrari depicting Dante recommending the M1 in 1912, and of a subsequent model memorably drawn by Pirovano racing down a railroad track with a steam train thundering alongside in 1920.

At this time, the corporate identity, such as it was, was a letter I enclosed in a C enclosed in an O. It was drawn by Olivetti and was in effect his monogram: Ingegnere Camillo Olivetti. These three letters would later ap-

Olivetti 1923

olivetti 1934

olivetti 1947

olivetti 1960

The Olivetti logotype has been through a number of transformations from a stylised signature to its present bold, rounded lower-case style

pear in other forms, for example laid out as a tall I followed by smaller C and O in a square box with the word Olivetti in capitals underneath as the badge on a 1935 typewriter. So this cannot be said to be corporate identity as we understand the term today. But this is no surprise since the idea of corporate identity had not yet lodged in the collective consciousness of business people. Indeed, Olivetti was in fact already somewhat ahead of the game.

DESIGN PATRONAGE

When Adriano Olivetti took over from his father to run the company from 1924 to 1960, he took steps to formalise the design structure. He introduced the concept of corporate image and identity, long before it was generally recognised as a business tool. Unlike AEG or IBM, which relied largely on a single figure (Peter Behrens, Eliot Noyes) to engender a design consciousness, Olivetti took a more heterogeneous approach that suggests a greater cultural confidence. In 1947, Pintori took another look at the hand-written Olivetti letters from Camillo's signature, that had first been applied to typewriters and later modified to appear as if typed on printed matter. He retained the letters all in lower-case and reworked them in a bold, slightly rounded typeface that remains the root of the logotype today. Towards the end of Adriano's reign, Olivetti adopted a symbol for the first time. Designed not by a graphic designer, and still less by a corporate identity consultancy, but by the product designer Nizzoli the symbol comprises two nested squares drawn in a

Detail of an early Olivetti typewriter showing Camillo Olivetti's monogram employed as the corporate symbol

Schawinsky designed the basic form of the modern logotype introducing a typewriter script appropriate to the company's products

The logotype was modified by 1950 when Nizzoli and Pintori comprised a formidable team of industrial designer and graphic designer

The 1930s logotype was used on printed matter in a similar manner to the modern logotype

single line. Nizzoli described its symbolism as a "Beginning without end".

The company continued under family control after Adriano's death in 1960, but design slipped down the list of priorities. The company recognised the situation and resolved it with the promotion of Renzo Zorzi, who had edited Olivetti journals and run its publishing operation, to the all-encompassing role of cultural co-ordinator. Zorzi had known Adriano and understood the ineffable principles by which he sought to nurture his company and its cultural contribution. *Under Adriano Olivetti's successor, Carlo De Benedetti, Zorzi had the authority he needed to institutionalise this early, essentially personal patronage. Zorzi saw that perhaps the only way that Olivetti could retain its essential spirit would be to set up a sort of evangelical administration at the very heart of the corporation that would exist solely to broadcast that spirit to Olivetti employees, to Italians and to the world at large.* Zorzi duly gained the necessary influence to establish such a department and imbued it with an intellectual depth that put it far in excess of such departments that are conventionally called "corporate communi-

cations" or "marketing communications" in other companies. As the history of Olivetti's design states, Zorzi "not only set up the appropriate organisational structure for this division, he also created the theoretical and abstract foundations for defining the purpose and necessity of a corporate image policy in a modern company".

Zorzi still heads the Corporate Image Department despite some brief irregularities in his tenure. Its aim now as then is to gather into one department control of all activities that give Olivetti its material expression. There are two product design divisions. In addition, Zorzi set up a department of graphic design under Roberto Pieraccini and then Hans von Klier that comprised typeface design, corporate identity, and an office with responsibility for cultural activities. This last department, to which Zorzi serves as a consultant to this day, co-ordinated a wide range of exhibitions from icons of Italian culture, to fine art, to thought-provoking shows of contemporary design (the "New Domestic Landscape" exhibition of Italian design at the New York Museum of Modern Art

Olivetti put its logotype in the window of its store on New York's Fifth Avenue (the Guggenheim Museum of the same era is on the same street)

The corporate symbol designed to accompany the lower-case logotype was by the industrial designer Marcello Nizzoli in 1956

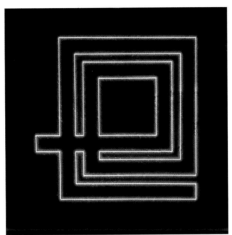

Save Our Planet Save Our Water

Olivetti has commissioned well-known artists, such as Roy Lichtenstein, to produce work for specific campaigns

The symbol could be employed on company structures where it would be difficult to place the logotype

Olivetti's sponsorship of cultural events, usually with a strong Italian bias, are an important ingredient in its corporate personality

Olivetti's sponsorship of exhibitions is sometimes of direct relevance to its market

Franco Bassi's clean, abstract artwork shows the **Olivetti** logotype in the central position dictated in corporate identity guidelines

Olivetti's news magazine shows the company's concerns are culturally broad, drawing attention to sponsored exhibitions

LETTERA 32 OLIVETTI PER TUTTI

In advertising posters by Jean-Michel Folon, Olivetti permitted an artist to take an ironic look at their technology

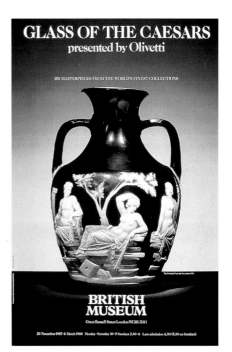

But more often, sponsorship has a less direct benefit through the general promotion of Italian culture through the ages

was one example). Although the subject matter is eclectic, each topic reflects some aspect of Olivetti's own culture.

MINIMUM LOGOTYPE

One action of the corporate identity department was again to modify the logotype. This time it was Walter Ballmer who considered playing with the letters, for example stylising the "tt" or "tti" to appear more abstract and technocratic. In the end, he limited himself to giving a further rounded and still bolder look to the letters. *This 1970 logotype, together with a palette of six colours and some guidelines on sizing and positioning, is intentionally a minimum around which Olivetti can build a visual language with the variety and spirit that is so much part of Italy. The fact that it is still in use today is an indication of its suitability.*

The corporate identity department has in effect three roles. Its principal purpose is to oversee implementation of the corporate identity according to the manuals produced in the 1970s by the Milan-based Anglo-Spanish Perry King and Santiago Miranda.

Secondary tasks include the control of the corporate image as it applies to Olivetti's office furniture and other divisions and to controlled companies using the Olivetti name such as those acquired in recent years by De Benedetti.

Von Klier and the industrial designers Bellini and Sottsass form an inner circle of regular, but still freelance, consultants who have shaped modern Olivetti. Within this framework, the company makes good use of other designers and artists, such as Glaser.

In two-dimensional design, there is no one figure today who fulfils the role taken by Sottsass and Bellini in product design. Giovanni Pintori came closest to this position during his long association with the company and with Nizzoli's products. His place was gradually taken by Franco Bassi. Bassi's rigorous training brought a sharp change. He introduced Olivetti's advertising to the electronic era with a use of geometry that was "very nearly moral", and a sparing use of colour. Writing about Bassi and Ballmer, Zorzi described Olivetti as

"an enterprise that has endeavoured for many years to create an identity of its

The 1970 logotype designed by Walter Ballmer makes the lettering bolder and more closely spaced

Detail of Ballmer's type specification for the 1970 logotype

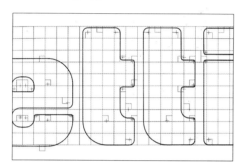

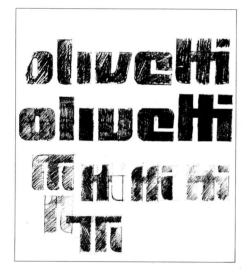

Ballmer considered alternative designs where, for example, the final letters were linked to form a "high-tech" device

own, with a homogenous visual style, in all fields of industrial design, architecture, interior decoration, printed matter, advertising and cultural activities ... the interaction of designer and company has been so close over a long period that it is often difficult to draw a dividing line."

The situation that Zorzi describes is typical of the equilibrium that Olivetti achieves with its designers.

FROM LOGOTYPES TO POSTERS

It seems perfectly natural that those who cope with the rigours and constraints of creating and overseeing the implementation of a logotype can also happily be set free to design posters and other artwork for the company. Ballmer's posters provided a necessary counterbalance to Bassi's abstractions. In his role as a corporate artist, Ballmer has employed what Zorzi calls "pictorial fantasy" and typographical experience in works that attempt to suggest some of the cultural effects associated with the use of the company product depicted. A drawing of a fragment of a keyboard shows four giant keys in an exaggerated perspective, for example, emphasising the link to Olivetti's industrial design as the selling point. King and Miranda's images were unlike the graphics of Bassi or Ballmer. Their approach was to set mysterious geometric shapes and symbols against a background distorted in their perspective, and often framed, like the paintings of the early Renaissance, although these symbols once again often had a didactic intent, most notably perhaps with the twisted crystal motif that was used for

1974 posters by Walter Ballmer who had created the modern form of the Olivetti logotype in 1970

the Design Process Olivetti exhibition and the accompanying book to illustrate the interconnection between Olivetti's design and cultural activities. In recent years, however, the elegance of the abstractions of Bassi and Ballmer and the allegory of King and Miranda has been interrupted by banal copy-heavy advertising, flagged with bold capital headlines in the undistinguished type that might be used by any corporation. In product design, the 1980s also saw some personal computers with little to distinguish them from the pack, notwithstanding the addition of some fine typewriters by Bellini.

The mid 1980s, like the early 1960s, marked another brief fall from grace.

Pressured by greater international competition, Olivetti turned its back on the values that had held good for three quarters of a century. Under new management, the design hierarchy was altered and decentralised with no co-ordinating authority overseeing activities in industrial design, graphic design and corporate identity. These unsettling moves were duly reversed and Zorzi was quickly restored to his familiar role as consultant on all matters cultural. As European companies do battle in the more competitive Single Market, Olivetti now has the opportunity to put to the test the real commercial merit of its design patronage.

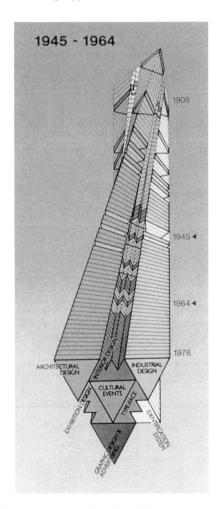

Artwork created by King-Miranda Associati to describe the corporate structure of Olivetti for the Design Process Olivetti publications

Elegant product design has long been a mainstay of Olivetti's design philosophy. These typewriters are by Mario Bellini

Modern artwork, such as this advertisement by Roberto Pieraccini, reflects the need to compete in tough international markets

Franco Bassi's modernistic poster style made the business of number-crunching look like fun

Corporate identity

SYNTHESIS

olivetti
Lexikon

Poster by Giovanni Pintori illustrates by its playfulness a continuous theme of the ease of use of Olivetti products

1ike many companies that carry a family name, Olivetti began with a logotype as a stylised signature. This has been through a number of modifications as the company has matured. But Olivetti's identity has continued to be characterised more by its attitude to design patronage in the broad sense. This is seen in continued excellence in the industrial design of products, the architecture of company buildings, and in the creation of individual posters and other graphic designs for various purposes more than in the monotonous repetition of a corporate mark.

PTT: PRIVATISED DUTCH NATIONAL POST AND TELEPHONE SERVICES

Client:
PTT Nederland NV, The Hague, The Netherlands

Corporate identity and design:
Studio Dumbar, The Hague, The Netherlands

Year:
1988-1989

to adapt the existing corporate identity of PTT as it changed from being a public utility to a private company; to increase consistency in the use of the identity at all organisational levels

The PTT identity has been applied with varying degrees of abstraction to everything from crockery to hot-air balloons

Stripes and bars from the identity form a variety of patterns that can be used in many different ways

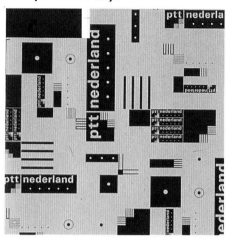

The elements of the PTT identity are sufficiently bold for use in black on printed collateral when colour printing is not possible

It may not be the most reliable measure of the success of a new corporate identity, but the Netherlands' most stolen canteen crockery is that of the post and telecommunications company, PTT. The reason for the attraction is that it does not in fact reveal the identity of the company. There are no words and no logo, simply shapes and colours that may be taken as decorative, but which, to those in the know (and this includes all of Holland), cannot fail to spell out P, T, T.

The crockery is the most liberated implementation of an identity of remarkable sophistication and subtlety designed by Studio Dumbar to signal the company's privatisation at the beginning of 1989. As a public company PTT had a formidable history of design patronage. In 1945, it established an aesthetics department, later rechristened Art and Design, headed by Ootje Oxenaar, whose other role in Dutch life has been to design many of the country's banknotes.

The high visibility of such designs—what could be more ubiquitous than a country's money in its people's pockets and its post and telephone boxes on their streets?—contributes greatly to the Dutch visual culture. Holland is almost unique not only for the way in which institutional patrons embrace Modernism today but for the fact that they have done so virtually continuously since the birth of Modernism itself.

The Dutch post office's own history of patronage began in 1912, a time of rich ferment in art and architecture in the country. At this time, Jean-François van Royen, then a company clerk, but trained in typography, first noted the poor design of the PTT's collateral and resolved to put matters right. This he did over thirty years by employing such avant-garde designers as Piet Zwart and Gerard Kiljan. One legacy today can be seen in the national post museum in The Hague where, to judge by the exhibit captions, visitors are expected to have an appreciation of such fine points of design as the merits of one Univers typeface over another.

After the Second World War (during which van Royen was interned and murdered), the PTT's art and design department continued to give commissions to the leading designers of the day such as Wim Crouwel and Jan van Toorn.

The three primary colours denote
PTT's post, telecommunications and
corporate divisions respectively in red,
green and blue

Company vehicles provide one of the
most visible implementations of the
PTT identity

The recent history of PTT design
began in 1981 when an identity was
introduced conceived jointly by Total
Design, the large, staid Amsterdam
consultancy then headed by Wim
Crouwel, and Tel Design, smaller and
more adventurous, where Gert
Dumbar was working. Its purpose
was to bring order to a corporation
that was growing and diversifying,
acquiring new departments in addition to 'Post' and 'Telecommunicatie'.
By 1987, Telecommunicatie had
grown still further and felt ready to
signal its maturity with its own revision to the 1981 identity. Without
referring to Art and Design, Telecommunicatie went to an advertising
agency with the job. Oxenaar learned
of the move, and suggested instead
that Total Design and Studio Dumbar
be asked to submit designs (the two
consultancies held copyright to the
earlier identity).

Around the same time, Wolff Olins
had been commissioned to take a critical look at PTT's overall image.
(One company director had apparently seen and admired the London
identity consultants' work for the
Dutch chemicals company Akzo.) The
report spoke of PTT's need to pre-

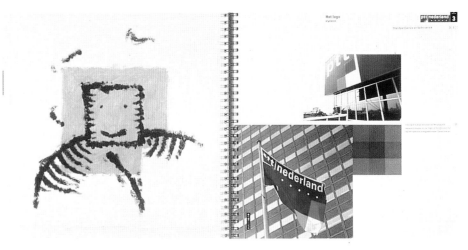

A double-spread from the manual showing the freedom with which art not
directly derived from the corporate
identity can be used

The red, green and "missing" squares arise from a grid of 16 squares that comprise the main PTT box

Manual illustrations by Berry van Gerwen and photography by Lex van Pieterson indicate the lightheartedness of the new identity

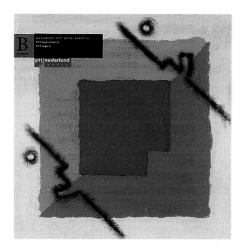

The small blue square on this red PTT logotype acts as a quiet reminder that

PTT Post is a division of PTT Nederland

sent itself more commercially. Although Wolff Olins was aware of PTT's rich graphic heritage and would have striven to retain it, there can be little doubt that if it had gone on to execute the new identity, the image would have become less Dutch.

Total Design's Telecom proposal used dots and dashes of the type that have appeared like a rash among such companies in recent years. Dumbar devised a logotype that "updated" the Telecommunicatie green, incorporating a silhouette of a satellite dish into the T of Telecom. However, work was interrupted with the appointment of a new managing director, Wim Dik, from Unilever.

Unilever is not known as a leader in design, yet Dik came to PTT with a clear understanding of the role that design could have as the corporation underwent privatisation. One preparatory manoeuvre was once again to reinforce the relation of Post and Telecom to each other and to the PTT holding company. This time there was no contest. Having proven their worth with the Telecom project, Studio Dumbar won the job. Total Design protested, saying they were denied a fair competition. Relations have since

been rather frosty, although Total continues to design Holland's post office interiors.

CONTINUITY AND MODERNITY

"The brief was to find a system where the different departments in PTT—Telecom, Post, holding—should be one family, but should be different," explains Oxenaar's assistant Ada Lopes Cardozo. *"It had to be based on elements of the old house style which were the colours, the Univers type, and the square as a building block. At first sight, this is perhaps not very promising. Yet the colours were the primaries and the geometric elements were two of the platonic shapes. These building blocks were to prove versatile indeed."*

The key breakthrough was what Dumbar staff call the deconstruction sketch, by Ton van Bragt, the last in a long series of drawings separating, rescaling and layering the design ele-

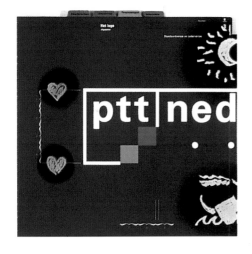

Much of the PTT literature is printed not using standard process colours but using the distinctive red, green and blue primaries of the principal PTT groups. This has the useful effect of making PTT equipment leap off the page. The special printing technique could be used in other literature in an extremely subtle implementation of the corporate identity

The identity manual comprises four volumes held in a box that features the core element of the PTT corporate logotype

ments. Dumbar comments that the design was "totally anti-clarity because clarity can be very boring. This brings the new clarity of uniqueness, with dogmatic figures that you can play with in a non-dogmatic way. It's remarkable what other design groups come up with."

Because the deconstruction occurs from a starting point of a grid of squares, it is hard for observers not to see something of De Stijl in the patterns that result. Dumbar designer Henri Ritzen explains:

> "The logo is built on a grid and the grid has basic forms—the circle and the square. The circle and square are elements that you can use in the logo and also elsewhere away from the logo, for special reasons such as on a page to position a headline or a photograph or on the side of a building."

The most closely controlled set of variations occurs in the three logotypes for PTT Post, PTT Telecom and the holding company, called PTT Nederland. Each has the letters p, t, t in a modified Univers 65 typeface set in white in a colour square box to the left. Adjoining the box and spaced from it by a white rule is a box three units long. Into this rectangle go the

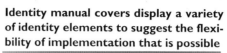

Identity manual covers display a variety of identity elements to suggest the flexibility of implementation that is possible

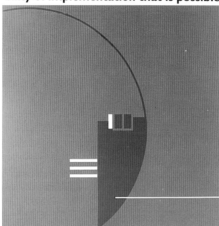

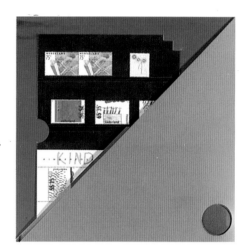

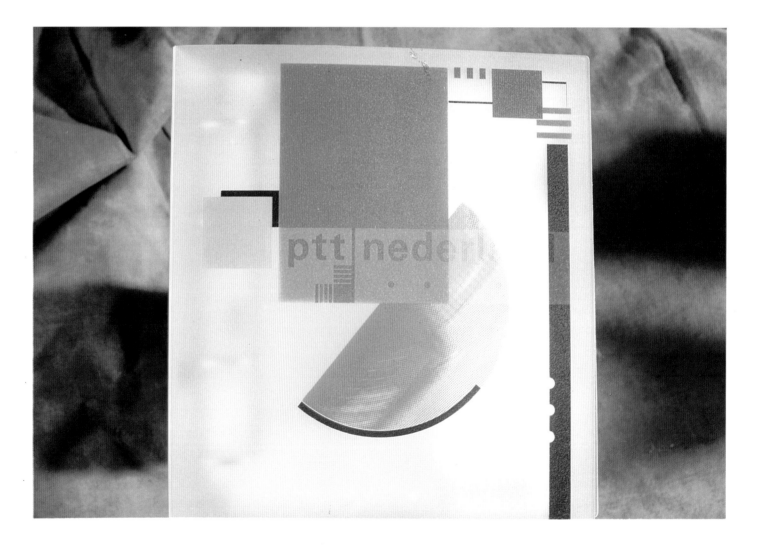

The elements of the identity can also be used with great sophistication.

Here they are layered to create a refined collage

PTT flags flutter along the Thames outside London's Design Museum to celebrate an exhibition on the Dumbar corporate identity

division titles and a row of five dots spaced according to the square grid. These are used as a registration convenience when affixing subtitles such as department names. The dots also hint at the Morse of telephony and the perforations of stamps but at neither as blatantly as in many similar companies' logos.

Unified Identity System

The boxes are red for Post, green for Telecom, or blue for the five other divisions. The square box is effectively divided into a grid of 16 smaller boxes, three of which are made explicit in the bottom right-hand corner of the Nederland identity, where small red and green "signal boxes" serve as a reminder that Post and Telecom are important constituents of PTT. A third white box is also bitten out of the PTT square. This looks awkward at first, as if Dumbar might have preferred that PTT had three major divisions, but this nick in the otherwise regular logotype box is an important identifier as well as a hint of the deconstructions possible in other circumstances.

In the case of the Post logo, the green box disappears and the red one is swapped for a blue box indicating that Post is still a part of PTT Nederland. The equivalent happens with the PTT Telecom logo. Where the logos can only be reproduced in a single colour, the box colours are distinguished from the ground colour by vertical and horizontal hatching.

The PTT Telecom identity adapted for use as a road sign at the entry to company premises

The **PTT** identity serves as a flagpole from which a company division title can hang like a banner from a key line of dots

The identity's origin in van **Bragt**'s "deconstruction sketch" is seen to good effect in abstract arrangements of identity elements

DEGREES OF FREEDOM

This much is non-negotiable. From here on freedom is granted in increasing doses by means of a tiered system devised by an American at Dumbar, Dawn Barratt. It is the play between the rigidity of the logo itself and the flexibility possible in other PTT design work that marks the Dumbar identity out from what a conventional identity consultancy might have produced.

> *"It was difficult for PTT to accept this contradiction; it also took them a long time to understand that this is not just a colour with typography and a name in it, but it is the logo," says van Bragt. "What's typically PTT is that you have a lot of colour and a little type. Like post offices the world over, the field of colour in which the identity sits is a distinguishing feature, a legacy of the days, well before corporate identities and professional graphic designers, when letter boxes were first boldly painted. It is a reminder that, apart from its money, the image of the national post and telephone company is probably the most powerful visual expression of a country's design."*

The flexible structure for design based on the identity has four levels.

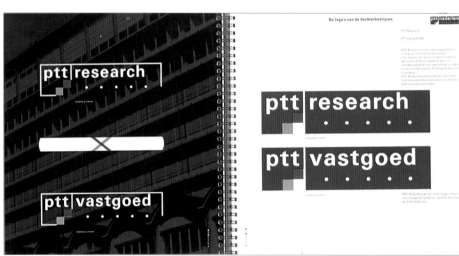

The lower case letters, p t t, are based on a modified Univers 65 typeface

The colours and formal elements of the PTT identity can be used decoratively without explicit reference to the company

The lowest is for in-house departments who want to knock out a quick brochure; the highest is when Art and Design asks one of Holland's many young design groups to respond to a brief for a special project. The rules are laid down in a style manual, a weighty but refreshingly light-hearted four-volume set printed occasionally in process colours but more often in the three PTT primaries. This is in order to make PTT accessories stand out in the photographs, but there is potential for the subtlest implementation of all of the identity by reproducing other full-colour material in this way.

The flexibility ensures that the PTT's very being pervades Dutch life. Its buildings, many of them conveniently constructed with a ready-made grid of glass curtain walling, support variations on the design. PTT trains have logos of different sizes stamped across them at wild angles. PTT uniforms are less institutional; company sportswear is even sold to all customers. The company is no less remarkable in its use of talented industrial designers, in particular the Leiden firm, Ninaber Peters Krouwel, which designed rural letter boxes and ingenious staff lapel badges. Lapel badges,

workmen's tents, phone cards, a flag —all vary the theme, not merely carrying the unadorned rubber-stamped logo. The phone cards have become something of a platform for young designers who win commissions from the PTT to commemorate notable events in individual graphic designs. Some are now collectors' items. And then of course, there are the coffee-cups that are tempting a new breed of designer kleptomaniac.

With the company strategy confidently decreed by Dik, and with his trust in Oxenaar and Dumbar, PTT is proof that a large and ambitious company with eyes on European expansion need not shun its local heritage. Says Ritzen:

> *"The Dutch belief in design is because of companies like PTT, and companies look like PTT because of the Dutch belief in design. It's impossible to separate the two. It's the guts to do it that's important."*

Set alongside a traditional postmark, the PTT lettering appears modern without being mannered

It is possible to break the rules of the identity manual, as when the grid is tilted at an angle and blown up to huge proportions on a post train

At night, this **PTT Post** building incorporates windows as well as identity elements into a dramatic geometric light composition

SYNTHESIS

the corporate identity is a subtle and sophisticated kit of parts that may be assembled in various ways to suit a large variety of applications and implementations. This allows subsequent design consultants unprecedented freedom to create designs for specific projects within the identity guidelines. Both in appearance and in this flexibility the new corporate identity upholds the tradition of the **PTT** before privatisation as a patron of design and perhaps the leading creator of **Dutch** visual culture.

LONDON UNDERGROUND

Client:
London Underground Ltd, London, Great Britain

Corporate identity and design:
Henrion, Ludlow and Schmidt, London, Great Britain

Year:
1984-present

to rationalise signs, maps and other passenger information in compliance with corporate identity criteria that aim to present the London Underground as a more modern and responsible organisation

Examples of passenger information literature using the New Johnston alphabet in various weights

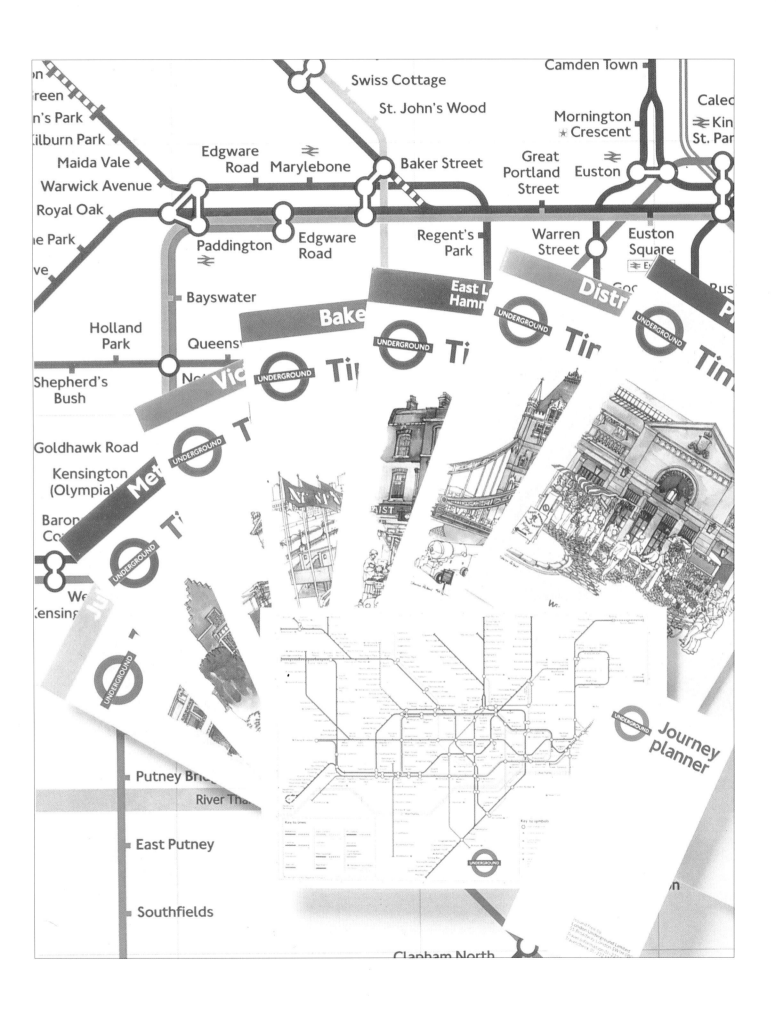

Some signs from the 1970s used **Old Johnston** type in favour of a more legible lower-case font and were poorly laid out

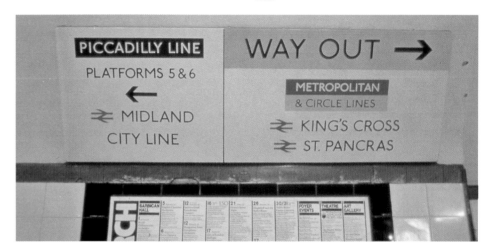

Standardised signage makes navigation easier for passengers in busy stations where Underground lines and British Rail services connect

the London Underground is the world's oldest urban transport network and one of its most complex. There are more than 200 stations on the dozen different lines that criss-cross the British capital. They differ greatly. Some are deep underground; others are on the surface. Up to six lines intersect at some; others are quiet rural halts. To devise an identity system to unify the network and make it comprehensible for the millions of passengers who use it each day is, it might be thought, challenge enough.

But there is also the Underground's history to take into account. The network began as separate companies, each operating its own private line. At one time, you even had to obtain two tickets for a single journey across London if that journey required a change from one line to another. Some of this legacy is still visible today. Stations reflect not just the era during which they were built but sometimes also the house style of their line. In particular, the Metropolitan Line which runs from the City far out into the suburbs north-west of London cherishes an independent heritage. Opened in 1863, it was the

London Underground is a large and complex transport network requiring a comprehensive corporate identity manual and other literature

Poorly assembled roundels on stations did a disservice to this elegant symbol that is central to Londoners' image of the Underground

first line and still regards itself as more of a "proper railway" than the others.

Different lines had different liveries and their stations had different ideas about layout and signage. So *when the independent lines merged at the beginning of the century, each came with its own visual heritage. Much was done to achieve unification during the 1920s and 1930s when the first coherent design policy was instigated on the Underground.* It was under Frank Pick, the managing director of both buses and Underground railway in the 1920s, that the London Underground acquired its influential identity with the famous roundel as its crowning glory.

There are in effect three layers in the archaeology of the London Underground: its "prehistory" as independent railways; the Pick era; and finally the post-war period that has seen a sequence of more or less minor modifications to Pick's vision with consequences that were generally banal (with the exception of competent work by the Design Research Unit on the new Victoria Line).

As if this were not complex enough, London Underground is today part of London Transport. It connects both with London Transport's own bus service and with British Rail's Network Southeast. Any visual identity must complement these systems as well as meet its own needs.

HERITAGE AND MODERNITY

This uniquely convoluted situation is both intimidating and inspiring to those who must work with it. The principal players are design manager Paul Moss, Christopher Nell, environmental and product design manager, and Corynne Bredin, corporate identity manager. Bredin acknowledges:

> "We have a wonderful history but an awful lot of very disparate design issues, projects and parts of identities."

The principal design consultancy working with Bredin on the London Underground corporate identity is Henrion, Ludlow and Schmidt. Chris Ludlow has no doubts as to the significance of the association:

> "It's part of world urban transport heritage, never mind London."

Examples of how station names should and should not appear in London Underground roundels

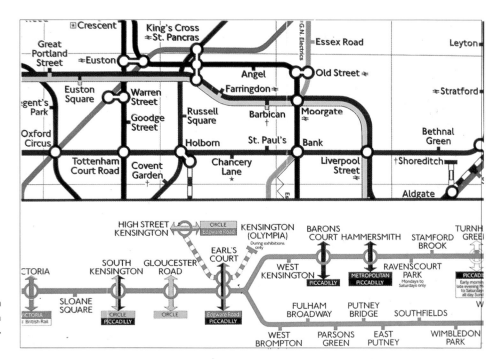

Underground line diagrams in train carriages (right) were inconsistent with the full system diagrams on station platforms (above)

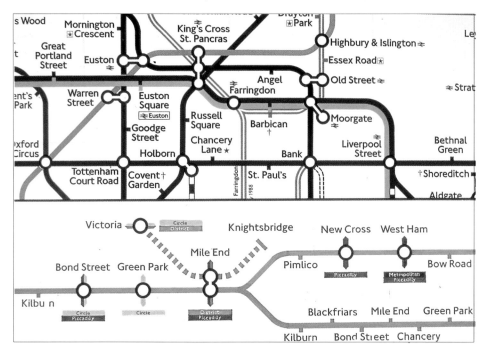

Henrion, Ludlow and Schmidt proposed to rationalise the line and system diagrams with common colours and typography

Some station signs of the 1970s used a black background to the roundel and were badly positioned making them hard to discern

Other signs sacrificed important elements of the historic identity. Here, the blue bar of the traditional roundel has been simplified to red

Service improvements are notified to passengers using entertaining posters that take liberties with the visual elements of the Underground map

Such posters are not allowed for within the identity standards but if executed with care do little damage to the overall appearance

Henrion, Ludlow and Schmidt were commissioned to produce a signage study in 1984. They found that the company's in-house architects were working from inadequate and outdated documentation as they equipped new stations. Despite good intentions they could not help but break the company's own guidelines thanks in part to historical anomalies such as the fact that different departments had responsibility for commissioning and reviewing signs.

Henrion, Ludlow and Schmidt recognised that complete consistency would probably never be attainable. The designers therefore proceeded to devise a rational, evolutionary signage system for use when outdated existing signs were to be replaced, not for wholesale changeover which would not have been achievable.

Of necessity, this work involved a graphic treatment of the roundel, the basic combination of a red circle with a blue horizontal bar that is the London Underground symbol. Thus a signage project began to metamorphose into a corporate identity project. Two years after they had started work on the Underground signage, Henrion, Ludlow and Schmidt approached the company's marketing department to petition for greater involvement.

Their involvement has indeed intensified. One designer left to take charge of the signage programme for the Underground. Henrion, Ludlow and Schmidt produced volume after volume of slim booklets, each addressing a particular aspect of the company's identity. By 1987, London Underground was in possession of a complete signage manual and a number of identity booklets.

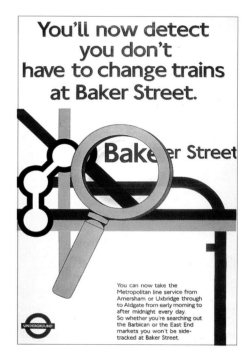

The magnifying-glass here is a reminder that Baker Street was Sherlock Holmes's fictional address

The standard colours for the various lines of the Underground were doubled in some cases with warning and information sign colours

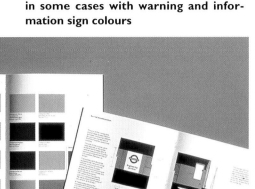

The famous London Underground map requires occasional modification as new connections are introduced

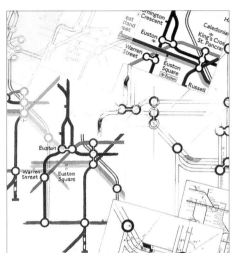

The London Underground identity is of primary importance to passengers, but company stationery has also been standardised

AFTER THE FIRE

But in the following year came an event that was to reshape company attitudes far more than any design change. *The King's Cross fire in 1988 had a cathartic effect on corporate culture. The obstruction and bureaucracy of jealous departments were largely swept aside and new board level management was installed. A new statement of policy placed safety, quality and efficiency uppermost.*

Corynne Bredin's appointment in 1989 followed shortly after. She retained Henrion, Ludlow and Schmidt and gave them additional responsibilities.

"They have a very rare logical approach," says Bredin, *"a strategic and methodical way in which they can assimilate a vast amount of information and convert it into a logical, informative, simple solution."*

Fortunately, London Underground's new-found management principles were in close accord with the design direction already being pursued. Indeed, realisation of this had a powerful effect in the upper echelons of the company. "It has given Design Management more meaningful authority

Models showing developments in train livery. The plain aluminium is clean and modern and distinct from paint or enamel finishes elsewhere

The final proposal, showing trains in the colours of different lines, is impractical because some trains run on more than one line

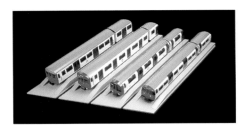

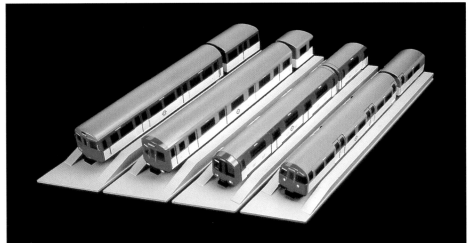

within the organisation," says Bredin. Henrion, Ludlow and Schmidt's identity strategy has centred on the rationalisation of existing devices such as the roundel, the colours that denote the Underground lines, and typography. The corporate identity standards published to date cover such discrete areas of activity as the roundel, train interior graphics, stationery, etc. It is intended that these standards will be interpreted onto interactive computer disks in order to provide a more user-friendly way of familiarising staff with the new guidelines.

One important move was to clarify colour usage. The designers knew that the key to passenger navigation lay in the distinctive colour allocated to each Underground line. They therefore discouraged the use of these colours—even of the "right" colour for a station—for decorative purposes. For reasons of economy, however, they standardised the doubling of some of the colours for general and safety signage where there was little likelihood of confusion. Piccadilly Line blue and Central Line red are also corporate house colours. Circle Line yellow is used for

The London Underground map has been extended and modified through the decades but remains true to the schematic original of 1931

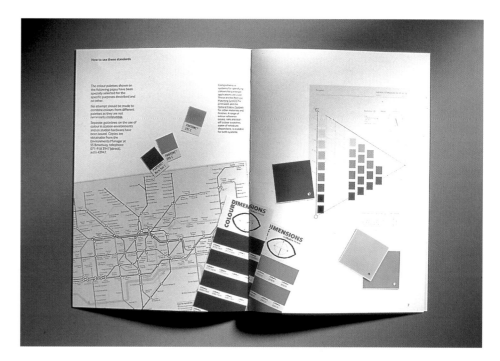

The exact colours for Underground lines and signage are specified and printed in a colour standards booklet

A train interior sign shows the use of New Johnston in upper and lower case with colours signifying different types of messages

Platform line diagrams must show both station names and the lines that intersect there with maximum clarity

New trains carry the house red and blue of London Underground, colours which also serve to denote two of its principal lines

Old Johnston type is an important part of the London Underground design heritage. Elegant in upper-case, it is hard to read in lower-case

safety warning signs. They also took steps to ensure that colours appeared the same in print as on vitreous enamel signs.

Following these guidelines, re-signing proceeds on a station-by-station basis. First, a sign planner visits the station recording existing signs, fixings, and noting any "heritage signs" that may be present. These observations are taken together with comments from the Group Station Manager, who knows which parts of a station become congested, or can identify the need for a special sign to direct people to an outside sight of interest. The signs unit then prepares a new sign system according to the guidelines laid down in the manuals. If a particular problem cannot be resolved by recourse to the manuals, the signs unit brings the problem to Bredin. A typical difficulty is when low headroom in a station concourse limits the amount of information that can be displayed on a hanging sign. Eventually, Bredin approves the proposed sign layout and the signs themselves are prepared using a CAD system and sent to one of six approved manufacturers of vitreous enamel signs.

Some sites are easier to re-sign than others. New stations can benefit immediately from the wholesale implementation of the current identity system. Heritage sites on the other hand require a more sensitive approach. *The policy is not to save everything that is old indiscriminately but to preserve the best from the past. With fragments from many different periods of differing worth, this can become quite an exercise in industrial archaeology.* An apparently historic roundel at a particular station could be a later reproduction, for example. The design department must use its knowledge of which roundel and signage designs were contemporaneous with the station architecture in making their decision.

In the early 1980s, conservationist concerns took matters to the opposite extreme, introducing spurious decorative elements to signage

Directional signage has been made less ambiguous by ranging messages left or right if they direct people left or right

The old sign system used upper-case lettering exclusively despite its poor legibility for directional signs

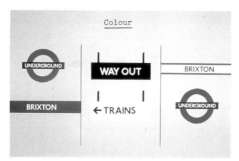

Henrion, Ludlow and Schmidt introduced lower-case lettering for directional signs and rationalised a palette of brighter house colours

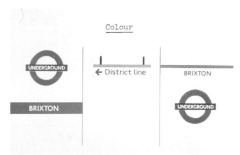

UNIFORMITY AND DEVOLUTION

The issue is not a simple one. At Baker Street, an important Metropolitan Line station, the company department responsible for making signs had taken it upon itself to design signs for the station platforms' brickwork arches with spurious historical detail. However, this is in contravention of a standards booklet on "heritage signs" soon to join those already published which will state the basic rule that while designated heritage signs are to be retained, there is no question of introducing reproduction signs in the historical style. While London Underground deliberates, half a dozen lobby groups—bodies such as English Heritage and the Twentieth Century Society—are breathing down its neck to make sure their special interests are respected.

The conflict between tradition and new demands is perhaps most acute in the typography used on the Underground. Aside from the roundel and the Underground map, the typeface now called Old Johnston, designed by Edward Johnston in 1916, is the most distinctive feature of the transport system. The sans serif face was used for centred messages in all capitals for station names and other signs. It had a pedigree and charm, but was unsuitable for extended messages. In lower-case, it appears quaint and is impossible to letterspace properly. The centring of the type caused confusion when an instruction was to go left or right.

"Centring is wonderful for certain simple layouts but for organising information it's not so helpful," comments Ludlow.

The new system makes use of a typeface designed by the London consultancy Banks and Miles, and christened New Johnston. Its usage follows more recent convention to convey messages unambiguously. Instructions relating to right-turn directions are ranged right and left-turn information is ranged left. Arrows are placed more logically than in the old system. Upper-case lettering survives only for station names on the roundel bars more for reasons of history than legibility. (For short messages such as these, recognition does not in any case depend upon readability.) Banks and Miles designed New Johnston in several weights, for headings,

Type samples from one of the identity manuals produced by Henrion, Ludlow and Schmidt

New Johnston was designed in several weights by Banks and Miles to meet the full range of London Underground's text requirements

New Johnston Bold
New Johnston Bold Italic

New Johnston Medium
New Johnston Medium Italic

New Johnston Light
New Johnston Light Italic

New Johnston Book
New Johnston Book Italic

 Alterations to Metropolitan Line services

Saturday 15th and Sunday 16th August

We're sorry, but because of engineering work there will be no Metropolitan Line trains between Baker Street & Finchley Road next Sunday. The Jubilee Line provides an alternative service between the two stations.

The Amersham service will run to and from Harrow-on-the-Hill, for connecting trains to London.

Please allow an extra 15 minutes for your journey.

This "heritage" roundel at a 1920s Underground station is one of those destined to be restored as part of the new signage system

Public information of a temporary nature is displayed on posters set out according to strict corporate identity guidelines

The London Underground roundel is given prominence in a broad white left-hand margin on printed matter

Leading fine artists are commissioned to produce colourful posters of scenes loosely associated with a station or London sight

The Art on the Underground campaign continues a tradition of artistic patronage pursued at times by London Transport

The posters occupy unsold advertising sites on Underground platforms and in tunnels

The identity manuals give detailed instructions to sign-makers and printers on how station names and other data should appear

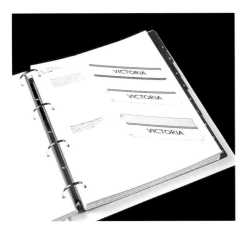

Standardisation is especially important in the network and line maps which must be readily intelligible to passengers

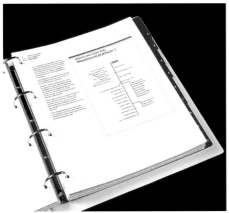

Important signs such as those showing the "Way out" have been given new emphasis in the Henrion, Ludlow and Schmidt signage system

poster messages and other uses. But London Underground had continued to use a variety of standard typefaces for body text in more detailed literature. One of Corynne Bredin's first actions was to undertake research which led to the commissioning of a body typeface, New Johnston Book, again by Banks and Miles, to complete the New Johnston family used exclusively by London Underground.

Bredin's quest for order amid the chaos comes at a time when the London Underground has undergone a management upheaval. This appears to some to be in tune with national government's ideology of privatisation of public services and it has led to a degree of devolution within the Underground. Line managers have gained a measure of autonomy and some regard their lines almost as brands. (A similar thing has already happened with urban bus services in Britain, with many companies serving one city.)

By definition, greater autonomy for individual lines means less consistency with any overall corporate identity. Individual line managers can already see it as not in their interests to co-operate with corporate design policy if it makes them appear as a part of a body from which they are trying to dissociate themselves.

The worst-case scenario for Bredin is that, in a few years' time, the manager of one of the newer, cleaner, more efficient lines will commission his own corporate identity with the brief that it should separate his service in the public's eye from the rest of the dirty, crowded, inefficient Underground. She is far from having finished her work to bring harmony and unity through more effective design to what was once a tangled nest of rival operators, and it seems that higher forces may yet turn the clock back a full century to reintroduce internal competition. The irony will be that both parties wish the travelling public to enjoy a more efficient service.

Chinatown by Underground
中國城
nearest station Leicester Square

UNDERGROUND

Chinatown
John Bellany ARA

one of a series commissioned
by London Underground

There is some friction between corporate identity and art commissioning, but in general posters conform to layout and type standards

SHOPPING on the UNDERGROUND

London Underground controls a vast retail empire which is in the process of acquiring its own branding

The diamond shape has been abstracted from the red-and-blue harlequin retail stripe as a central element in the retail identity system

A station photo booth carries the "harlequin" branding of London Underground's retail activities, a motif culled from old signs

Corporate Identity

SYNTHESIS

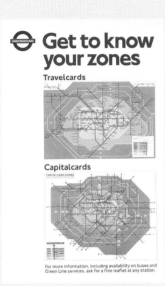

Get to know your zones

Travelcards

Capitalcards

CAPITALCARD ZONES

For more information, including availability on buses and Green Line services, ask for a free leaflet at any station.

More complex maps are now needed to explain the London Underground fare structure, but the famous network map serves as its basis

henrion, Ludlow and Schmidt recognised the history of London Underground's design patronage but also realised that old station signage and graphics were becoming confused. The redesigned signage system, the signs themselves, and other travel information honour the tradition of the service's corporate identity established in the 1920s, for example, by standardising the appearance of the famous red and blue roundel. But they also take into consideration aspects of safety and new technology and the client's marketing objectives and strategies.

GLOSSARY

brand
distinguishing name and/or symbol of a product or service or range of products or services

brand identity
visual appearance used to distinguish a brand

branding
the process of conferring a brand identity upon a brand

brief
documents and discussions between a client and a design consultancy that describe a design problem

client
term used by a design consultancy to refer to the corporation that has commissioned it

collateral
secondary material that bears a corporate identity, for example company stationery

consultant/consultancy
term describing an independent group of designers who work for a variety of clients on a project basis

copyright
term describing the ownership of a creative work. In the case of the design elements of a corporate identity, this usually belongs to the client

corporate culture
a cliché term describing aspects of a company's demeanour and behaviour, covering such elements as staff morale, staff-customer interaction, business ethics and industrial relations

corporate identity
the visible expression of a corporation's personality or intended personality

corporate reputation
an umbrella term used to describe a company's attitude to broad concerns such as the environment, ethical investment, political neutrality etc

element
part of a corporate identity, for example a grid, particular colours or typefaces, that may be used in varied fashion in combination with other elements

equity
jargon term used to describe the inherent value to a company of a corporate identity or other visual device

font
see type

grid
a spatial arrangement used as a framework for graphic design

house style
a way of doing things, in particular producing creative material, by or for a client within the terms of corporate identity guidelines

ident
abbreviation of identity, used especially in reference to television design

identity
shorthand term used to describe the visual elements of a corporate identity

implementation
process of applying a new corporate identity to all company material such as stationery, signs, buildings, vehicles and products

in-house
professional jargon describing design work carried out by designers employed by a company for use by that company

livery
term used to describe a corporate identity as applied to vehicles and uniforms

logotype (or logo)
a corporate identity or element of a corporate identity that is word-based rather than symbol-based, usually the company name (see symbol)

manual
book or books produced to describe the implementation of a corporate identity for use by a client's staff and suppliers

mark (also marque)
symbol and/or logotype that is the ever-present stamp of a company; usually the major element of a corporate identity

market research
survey of opinions of a company's customers, staff, competitors etc. that is used to inform the design of a new corporate identity

pitch, creative
a process in which design consultancies are invited by a client, preferably for a fee, to contribute sketches and creative ideas indicative of their capabilities for undertaking a project

pitch, credentials
a process in which design consultancies are invited to state their capabilities for undertaking a project

privatisation
government-legislated process of placing nationalised or publicly owned industries into private ownership; a major market for corporate identity design in the past decade

registered trademark
a mark, symbol, logotype or name that is registered by a company and legally protected for its exclusive use

research
see market research

signage
a system of informational signs that meets functional requirements using a visual vocabulary that is consistent with a corporate identity

symbol
a corporate identity or element of a corporate identity that is pictorial rather than word-based (see logotype)

type/typeface/typography
style or styles of lettering used by a company as an element of its corporate identity

visual audit
process usually undertaken by a design consultancy to ascertain the ways in which an existing corporate identity is used and misused by a client, in order to devise a new identity that resolves these shortcomings

vocabulary
a collection of elements that comprise a corporate identity; may sometimes be combined in different ways

BIBLIOGRAPHY

The Wolff Olins Guide to Corporate Identity, London, 1984

Cauzard, D., Perret, J., Ronin, Y. *Images de Marques, Marques d'Images,* Ramsay, Paris, 1989

Chajet, C., *Image by Design,* Addison-Wesley, Reading, Mass., 1991

Costa, J., *Imagen Global,* Spain, 1988

Olins, W., *Corporate Identity,* Thames and Hudson, London, 1989

Olins, W., *The Corporate Personality,* London, 1978